Heirloom Quilts from Old Tops

15 Contemporary Projects for Creating Quilts from Old Tops

Patricia J. Morris and Jeannette T. Muir

Published by

Krause Publications
700 East State Street
Iola, WI 54990-0001
www.krause.com

Please call or write for our free catalog of
publications. Our toll-free number to place an
order or obtain a free catalog is 800-258-0929
or please use our regular business telephone
715-445-2214.

Illustrations by Jan Wojtech, unless otherwise indicated.

All before photography by
Jeannette T. Muir.

All completed quilt photography by
James W. Muir.

Library of Congress Catalog
Number: 2001088585

ISBN: 0-87341-955-3

James W. Muir, photographer

Dedication

For Bill and Jim

Acknowledgments

Cherrill Louise Felmly (1893-1988) for 1940s fabric and quilt top donations before it was known that they would be needed

Paul Ferrigno, Moto Photo Portrait Studio, Maple Shade, N.J., for unlimited use of the studio

Bill Morris, Pitman, N.J., for his expert disassembly of *Gwendolyn Julie*, and for multiple chores

Jim Muir, Medford, N.J., for all photography and equipment handling

Julie Powell, Merion, Pa., for appraisal expertise

Kathlyn Sullivan, Raleigh, N.C., for counsel and advice

Toby Sullivan, Raleigh, N.C., for finding *Maude Isabel*

Jessie Weeks, Moorestown, N.J., for generous donation of her mother's fabric for use in *Maude Isabel* and others

Madge Ziegler, Newark, Del., for miscellaneous references

To the staff at Krause Publications for smoothing the way to publication

Foreword by Kathlyn Sullivan

The everyday events of our lives compel us to prioritize. We are always stashing away creative endeavors, because life interrupts us: a meal must be prepared, a child attended to, or a cow has wandered into the garden. Throughout our nation's history, it has been no wonder that thousands of quilt projects have never been completed. Today we make light of this reality by referring to those incomplete items as UFOs (unfinished objects).

The vast majority of old and/or unfinished quilt tops have at least some redeeming qualities: good color, difficult design, creative zest, delicious fabrics, or the historical reality of the social and economic contexts in which they were made. With these factors in mind, the tradition of recycle, reuse, and renew surges forward and with it the precious reconnection of the generations. Classic or unique, quilt tops are worthy of being creatively modified or completed as found.

I can think of no better experts than Patricia Morris and Jeannette Muir to guide the quiltmaker through this process of quilt renewal and rescue. Through them comes technical skill and experience along with decades of quiltmaking and teaching expertise. Both as teachers of quiltmaking and as quilt judges certified by the National Quilting Association, Pat and Jeannette have helped lay the groundwork of quiltmaking standards. Their work is proof that old top rescue is not only practical, but provides a superior vehicle for unique and creative application.

Table of Contents

Flower designs by W. C. Morris

General Introduction

After requests from readers for more *Worth Doing Twice* quilts and more technical information, we decided that further exploration of old quilt tops and the process of completing them was called for. And so ... *Heirloom Quilts from Old Tops*!

More and more often, quiltmakers show interest in old quilt tops and in salvaging them. For one thing, old quilt tops are considerably less expensive to acquire than old quilts. Even if the old quilt top requires a considerable amount of work to complete, you are intimately involved in completing the top (rather than simply collecting an old quilt), which makes it more your own.

With the approach used here, we don't become solemn over completing tops. Instead we maintain a light-hearted approach and don't get involved with museum-quality or actual heirloom tops. We

enjoy the work and face it on a practical level. Completing the quilt tops is a way of honoring our quilt fore-bearers without getting sentimental and gooey over the project.

Our interest began when we each purchased two old tops from the same vendor at the same show. Once we "tasted" the pleasure of completing the old tops, we were totally committed to the work — not to the exclusion of our other quiltmaking, but as a special part of it. Since that time, we have devoted many hours to various *Worth Doing Twice* projects, with Jeannette completing many, many tops.

In this volume, you will find photos of the old tops as they looked when they were bought and when they were finished. Also there are photos of, and directions for, contemporary quilts or wall hangings, each inspired by one of the old quilts.

For us this is a pleasurable activity, and we are devoted to getting other quiltmakers involved in this endlessly fascinating, challenging, and satisfying work.

$\mathcal{P}$urpose

There are many purposes for completing old quilt tops, and they fall in no particular order of preference. One of the reasons for doing this work is simply because you really enjoy it. This enjoyment can encompass any necessary repairs, careful designing or redesigning, and using the old top or pieces of old tops. The remaking can be done because you've unearthed a special treasure that you are really taken with. It's a top that you feel you must add to your collection for whatever reason.

You may also want to honor and perhaps remember the original top maker. This is done by completing the work, so the quilt may have a full and extended life. Instead of quilting an old top, you may choose to work with old blocks. When working with old blocks, the set of the blocks is an important element. The blocks may all be of the same type, clearly intended to be put together into a single quilt. On the other hand, the blocks may be of all patterns, sizes, and colors. Making a quilt of this hodge-podge of blocks can be lively and exciting and, as a bonus, thrifty.

Whether some people in the field approve of the process of remaking old tops or not, it is worth doing. Those who disapprove climb on their soapboxes and try to convince you to keep your hands off old tops (or quilts). They want to

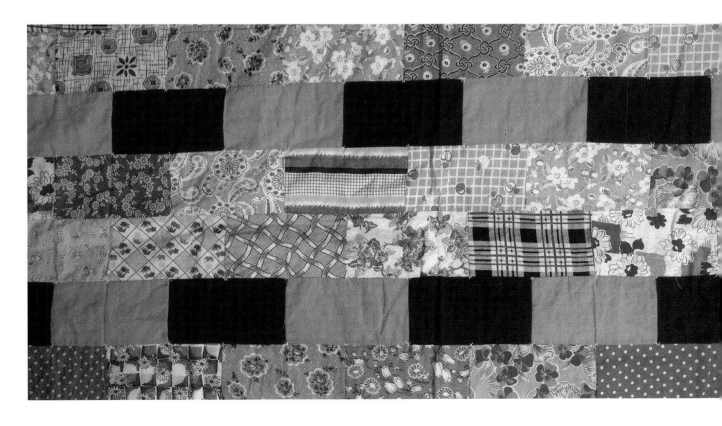

treat these as if they were sacred. Neither of us approves of tampering with museum quality quilts, beyond keeping them in reasonable "health." These are best left in the hands of the museum textile professionals. Despite the nay-says, we find it worth the work to save other old tops from extinction.

Another reason for completing old tops is the real satisfaction in doing so. As we've noted, collecting and completing old tops is far less expensive than collecting old quilts—though old tops, just like old quilts, are rising in price. When searching for old tops, the best bargains have been those that were made between the 1870s and the 1950s. But, interestingly enough, since our first book we've seen tops made in the 1970s and 1980s sell fast and easily and, for the most part, at extremely reasonable prices. So, while you purchase the old top, you might want to stock up on some "newer" old tops. Of course, if you're able to track down a top by a "name" quilt-maker, that would be a real find.

Using this book, we hope to recruit our contemporaries as well as other old top fans and collectors to complete the old tops. We would also like to spread interest to non-quilters. There is value in the inspiration that the old tops, completed or uncompleted, can provide for making new quilts or reproductions of old quilts.

One thing to remember is that we, as quiltmakers, need and want to make the best use of our quiltmaking time. Lots of our work is done while visiting, sitting in waiting rooms, watching television, and other pursuits that don't require our full attention. Some quilters are even able to stitch or unstitch while they are passengers in a car or on a bus or plane!

For those who are textile history students, the old tops can provide study pieces. Completed old tops, stabilized and preserved for future study, can be valuable historical pieces.

We learn from the old tops, and we preserve the past and carry it into the future. Old tops are good investments, and we find them a satisfying pursuit. The completed quilts should outlive the next couple of generations; they become part of our legacy.

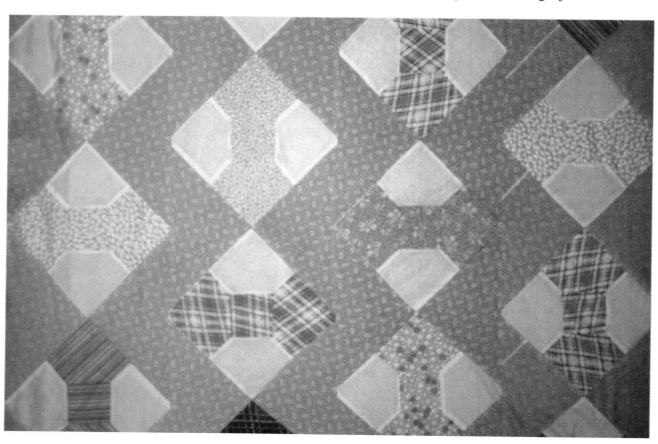

Frequent Technical Problems and Their Solutions

Once you find (wherever that may be) the old quilt top that you want to complete and determine that it is indeed worth completing, take a careful look at the top and check for the specific problems that need to be addressed. Some quilt tops have minor, easily fixed problems, while others, although still worth working on, have major ones. Some tops are nearly completed as they sit, while others may need to be carefully picked apart and reassembled.

Remember to carefully inspect every detail of the top to be certain you don't miss any areas that need attention. While it is one thing to repair and complete an old top, it is something else indeed to complete the work and then find you have missed an error somewhere, or worse yet, you have incorporated an error of your own during the completion process. To be sure any details you have noticed are not forgotten in the repair work, you might want to put a safety pin at that problem, or stick a piece of masking tape beside the problem detail. In any event, don't trust your memory; mark the spot needing repair.

It is surprising to see the various types of problems that appear in the old tops. Some of the problems you will see infrequently, while others crop up time after time. If you find that you enjoy completing old tops, you might want to learn or develop efficient methods for identifying problems and for dealing with common technical errors.

Listed here are problems we have most often encountered and how they were solved.

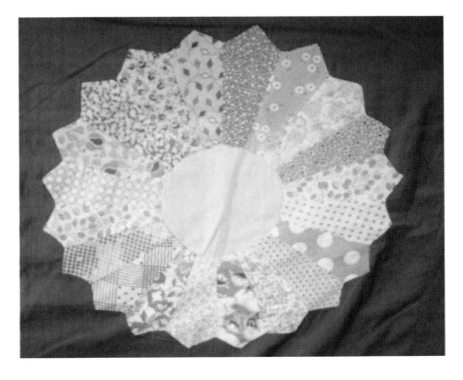

Appliqué:

Problem: *Frayed edges*

Solution: Carefully remove piece. Press, recut, prepare, and apply new piece.

Problem: *Poor workmanship*

Solution: Remove appliqué piece, recut, and apply new piece in place. Keep in mind that "poorly done" is in the eye of the beholder. Don't make unnecessary work for yourself if the appliqué is really satisfactory.

Borders:

See Chapter 12

Fabric:

Before you begin working with the fabric, Magic Sizing® and steam pressing are recommended for removing wrinkles and adding body.

Problem: *Fabric tears like paper*

Solution: This often happens with the typical brown fabric of the late 1800s, which was dyed with metallic-based dye. These pieces will have to be replaced.

Problem: *Bias edges and/or wiggly edges*

Solution: Be certain that the pieces are marked and cut to the proper size. Pin more frequently than usual when preparing to stitch.

Problem: *Brittle fabric*

Solution: If fabric tears easily, and it cannot be replaced, back the entire piece with lightweight, iron-on knit interfacing (following the manufacturer's instructions). Or cut 1/4" strips of interfacing and fuse them to the straight seam and cross-grain seam allowances only. (Bias edges will not tear.)

Problem: *Flaws*

Solution: It's your personal choice to leave it in place or replace it.

Problem: *Fragile/see-through fabric*

Solution: If a replacement cannot be found, back the entire piece with the lightest-weight, iron-on knit interfacing (following the manufacturer's instructions).

Problem: *Holes*

Solution: There is more than one way to approach this problem.

1. Appliqué something appropriate over the hole.

2. Cut the piece into two parts, cutting directly across the hole. Restitch the piece, so the parts of the hole are well within the new seam allowance. Use small machine stitches and a matching thread color. Press the seam open.

3. Determine if the piece is vitally needed. If the hole is very close to, or partially in, the seam allowance, carefully pick the pieces apart, recut, and restitch.

Problem: *Loosely woven fabric*

Solution: Replace the piece(s) with same-vintage fabric, if possible. Otherwise, follow suggestions for "Fragile/see-through fabric."

Problem: *Off grain*

Solution: Not fixable. Leave it and enjoy.

Problem: *Poor quality fabric*

Solution: Replace the piece if necessary. Any replacement fabric should be of good quality. Muslin, especially, frequently has to be replaced. Some muslins are loosely woven and gauze-like, while others are so heavy they seem almost like canvas. As with any replacements, the preferred fabric is that of the same vintage/period as other fabric used in the top, if at all possible.

Problem: *Soiled/stained*

Solution: Before deciding to use a replacement fabric, turn the fabric wrong side up to see if the reverse side looks to be without stain or soil and will solve your problem. If that doesn't help, try washing the fabric (see chapter 6).

Problem: *Stitching holes that remain after picking out machine stitches*

Solution: Use the fabric, if threads are not broken.

Laundering will help draw the threads together. If washing separate pieces, put the pieces in a hosiery (or other similar) bag so they won't be harmed in the process.

Piecing:

Problem: *Unavailability of replacement fabric*

Solution: Make color photocopies of the old fabric on new muslin

Problem: *Inadequate seam allowances*

Solution: You may have to pick the top apart and reduce the size of the pieces, being sure the templates are accurate and that you have a wide enough seam allowance on each edge. The seam allowances should be 1/4" on all sides. Doing this every time you need to create a seam allowance reduces the size of the piece, but you create a solid piece in the bargain.

Problem: *Inconsistent size of pieces*

Solution: Pick the work apart, remark (making all like-pieces consistent in size), recut, and resew. Make sure all new templates are accurate.

Problem: *Inaccuracy of intersections*

Solution: Pick the work apart in problem areas, recut, and restitch. If a large number of intersections do not meet, pick the whole top apart and then remark, recut, and restitch.

Problem: *Pleats, puckers, bubbles*

Solution: When you discover pleats, puckers, or bubbles stitched in along the seam line, pick the seam(s) apart, press, remark, recut, and restitch, eliminating the problem.

Problem: *Selvages*

Solution: If there are no puckers, as a result of the selvage being included in the seam allowance, the selvage can be used. However, if necessary, pick the top apart, remove the selvages, remark, recut, and restitch.

Problem: *Unstitched seams/ seams pulling apart*

Solution: See solution for inadequate seam allowances.

Thread:

Problem: Poor quality

Solution: Remove existing thread and replace it with good quality, regular sewing thread—not too thick or too thin. 100% cotton is recommended to protect cotton fabrics.

Top:

Problem: *Bias Perimeters*

Solution: Spray with Magic Sizing and press to help stabilize the top. Handle the top carefully to avoid stretching. Measure carefully across as well as both ends and sides, and, most importantly, across the middle and down the center. Add borders cut to size, and pin frequently when preparing to stitch borders.

Problem: *Inconsistent block size. This applies to quilt tops having blocks that are not the same size, purchased individual blocks of the same type (all pieced, all appliquéd, etc.), and purchased individual blocks of different types.*

Solution: Re-make the blocks. Keep in mind that either of the following solutions will probably result in a reduced size of the overall work.

When working with blocks of the same type, cut them to the same size or add a "frame" to each block, so you can cut all the blocks to the same size.

When working with blocks of various types, make, remake, or cut them to the same size; or stitch them together with filler blocks (of whatever size is needed to make a rectangular or square quilt).

Problem: *Top does not lie flat*

Solution: Picking apart the entire top and remaking it is probably the solution. The problem is generally the result of overall poor workmanship.

Workmanship:

Problem: *Overall construction is poorly done*

Solution: Pick apart, size all pieces, remark, and restitch. Here is another instance where judgment should be tempered with common sense. Don't redo that which can be reasonably retained.

Note: Tops that seem beyond repair due to paint stains, animal accidents, or whatever, should not automatically be considered trash. They may be "sacrificial tops," ones where the full top is so poor or irredeemable that it cannot be restored, but where certain fabrics in it are in good shape and can be used to repair other, more fixable tops.

Keep your eyes open for all of the above-discussed problems before determining what needs to be done to complete the top. But don't confine yourself to looking for only these problems; others that we have not run across may be lying in wait.

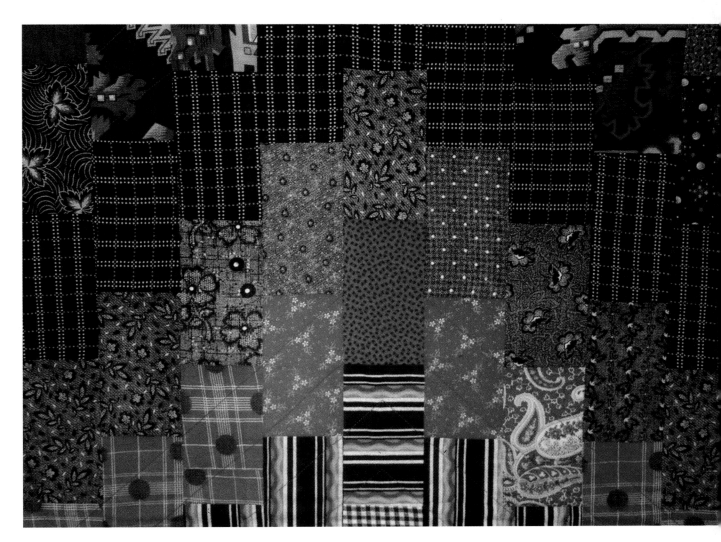

3 Basic Visual Problems

Just as there are technical problems with an old quilt top that need handling, so also will you encounter basic visual problems that require attention. Some of the visual problems are caused directly by technical problems, while other visual problems have their own origins.

One of the visual problems concerns the layout or set. This usually happens with sampler-type quilts and their balance. Whether dealing with an old top that is pieced or one that is appliquéd, the block layout should be arranged so that the layout is balanced. This balance applies to color, visual weight, fabric scale, and arrangement of similar or non-similar blocks. If the balance is off, you will feel, as you view the top, as if you are leaning to one side.

If there is trouble with color placement, the piece may need to be rearranged. This will probably require picking apart some of or the entire top, in order to reach a pleasing color arrangement. In discussing color, contrast has to be considered. The lack of contrast will cause all of the pieces to seem to melt together. On the other hand, too much contrast in the color will seem to allow the stronger ones to take over the quilt top.

A seemingly inappropriate choice of fabric colors is a quite basic problem and one that may need a considerable amount of work to correct—if it is at all possible to correct it. If just one or two fabric colors create a problem, you can pick the top apart and replace the troublesome fabrics with more appropriate choices. If all of the fabric colors are causing a visual problem, some consideration needs to be given as to whether or not the top should be completed. Despite inappropriate fabric color choices, the decision may be to go ahead and finish the top, especially if the top brings a smile to your lips or a song to your heart.

Another visual problem may be sashing and border size. If the sashing and border are too big (wide), they may easily be cut down in size to better fit the quilt top. If the sashing and border are too small (narrow), they can be replaced with fabric of the same period. This amount of old fabric may be difficult to find and expensive to purchase. In the instance of the too-small sashing and border, the choice may be to leave it as it is, complete the top, and live with the visual problem.

If the top causes a visual problem, because it doesn't lie flat, and if the problem can't be corrected technically (or without too much effort), the choice may be to stretch and block the top and then to baste it firmly before tackling the quilting. Ruffled borders, puckering, and sashing and border straightness can be corrected technically.

When choosing an old top, it's important to assess both the technical and visual problems while the decision is being made to complete the top. Remember the quilt, both as a top and as a finished piece, should provide you with enjoyment. If the work required to complete the top outweighs your pleasure in the finished product, you may wish you had more carefully considered your original decision to proceed.

*H*unting down old tops involves various things, some of them monetary. There are certain expenses involved in completing old tops. The first is the cost in obtaining one. If you're willing to hunt through real estate sales, yard sales, and auctions, you may be able to come up with a good bargain. On the other hand, if you (as we) don't choose to go grubbing through these sources, the best place to get the old tops is from quilt show vendors. They are usually willing to search around and come up with an interesting inventory of old tops. They know where to look and who to talk to. Their connections are good, and they are willing to dig around so the rest of us will have a wide selection of tops to choose from. With any luck, the vendor should be able to supply a provenance for the top in which you are interested.

One tip: Check out the vendors at a show as soon as the show opens on the first day. There is quite a bit of competition for the old tops, and it is steadily growing. If you see a top you like, but you're not quite sure about it or the price doesn't seem right, keep looking and perhaps you will find one you can't live without. You can always go back to one seen earlier, and hope it's still available.

Of course, a vendor may charge more than you'll pay when you directly discover the old top yourself. When you do choose to shop from the vendors, be reasonable and determine how much you are willing to spend, setting yourself a rational budget and taking into consideration the work needed to complete the top. Of course, many factors will enter into your decision to purchase: age of the top, condition, size, and so on, including the feeling that the top is right for you.

Once you have purchased an old top, you may find that you need some fabric to complete it—for instance, if one of the pieces used throughout the quilt has not held up and must be replaced. If additional fabric is needed, you may find fabric of the same vintage. But, keep in mind that period fabric is narrower than today's fabric, and can be quite expensive. Also, be certain that any vintage fabric you find is in good shape before you invest in it.

One alternative to using vintage fabric is to purchase reproduction fabric, which is available in many different fabric periods. Complete quilt shops will carry fabric from most periods currently being reproduced.

You can choose to throw caution to the wind and simply repair or replace the vintage fabrics (that are causing problems in the old top) with today's new fabric. The big problem here is that the new fabric has to be carefully chosen, or you will entirely lose the flavor of the old top. If you choose to go this route, search carefully with an eye to print scale, tints and shades, and color strength. If you use these modern fabrics with care, you may be able to have a strong, completed top without losing too much of the original charm of the old quilt top.

Another source of vintage fabric is a "sacrificial" top, one that has some usable areas, but overall can't be repaired enough to be happily completed.

The overwhelming reasons for finding and completing an old quilt top are that you like the piece, get enjoyment from choosing it, and find satisfaction in working on it.

5 *Getting Ready*

(*Assessing the Top/Advance Preparation*)

Before doing anything with your quilt top, photograph it and document any information you may have on it. Even though you carefully looked at the old quilt top before you purchased it, once your decision has been made you have automatically made a commitment to that top, and it's time to fully assess it in new ways.

Screen the entire top and each individual piece as we've indicated; flag problems with masking tape or safety pins. If you feel the process is going to be a protracted one, or the top has multiple areas to be flagged, or you haven't yet washed the top, it's probably better to use safety pins and reserve the use of masking tape for the pre-washed top or one that has fewer problem areas to be marked.

After you have evaluated the top and spotted the areas needing attention, your first job is to launder the top, if this hasn't been done previously. Use a soap specifically developed for laundering quilts. Most quilt shops carry one or more non-phosphate detergents or soaps. If you

don't have a shop reasonably close to you or your local shop doesn't carry any of these products, you can order them through a mail order source. After washing, rinse the top thoroughly.

Provided it is in good condition, the clean, wet top can be dried in an electric or gas dryer. Set the dryer to the delicate cycle, and use low heat. Before the top becomes overly dry, remove it and complete the drying process on a flat surface. Draping it over double clotheslines, either indoors or outdoors, can also dry the top. If drying outdoors, don't hang the top in direct sunlight.

Jeannette prefers to wash in gentle cycle and dry in gentle cycle. Pat favors washing the top by hand, and drying the top by hanging, avoiding machines altogether. Pat's preference may seem old fashioned, but she thinks it's safer and easier on the old top.

Do be aware that there are those who are against washing an old top. But neither of us wants to spend time working on something dirty, so we wash them before beginning

the work and accept whatever new problems this may present. What's the worst that can happen? During the laundering process, the entire top may disintegrate leaving you with pieces you can't complete into a quilt! However, the pieces that do survive can be used to repair other old tops. This is just the chance you take when you wash an old top, and we choose to take that chance.

If the quilt still has an odor after it has been cleaned, washed, and dried, place it unfolded in a plastic bag with a bar of unwrapped Safeguard® soap, and tie the bag shut. The length of time the quilt needs to be kept in the bag depends on the size of the quilt and the degree of the odor. Check for freshness after a couple of days, and repeat the process as needed.

If you determine you need to pick the top apart, do that process carefully. Then, use Magic Sizing or spray starch on both sides of each piece and steam press, then remark the piece. After the entire top is completed, wash it and the marking will wash out.

For any quiltmaking project, there are various tools and supplies that help the work progress easily. Following is a list of tools that you will find helpful in doing the projects in this book.

ADHESIVE BANDAGES:
Better to be safe than sorry, so be prepared for accidents.

BASTING SAFETY PINS:
Size #1, non-rusting safety pins are the tool of choice.

BATTING:
A matter of personal choice involving the look you want the finished product to have and the batting you like working with best.

BINDING CLIPS:
These hold the binding smoothly and securely while it is being hand stitched to the back of the quilt. They save being jabbed, as that can happen when straight pins are used.

EMBROIDERY FLOSS:
Floss is used to repair embroidered quilt tops as well as

to make new tops. It can also be used to embellish a quilt and to sign it. We prefer DMC® floss.

EMBROIDERY HOOP: Use it to hold fabric securely when making or repairing embroidered or appliquéd blocks.

EVEN-FEED/PLAID MATCHER/WALKING-FOOT ATTACHMENT: Most helpful in machine quilting your piece, it feeds the layers through evenly.

EXTENSION CORD: A handy, "just in case" piece of equipment.

FABRIC SCISSORS: A good pair of sharp scissors is needed for cutting fabric only. We've found Gingher® makes the best scissors currently on the market.

IRON: A heavy iron with steam and spray functions.

IRON-ON INTERFACING AND NON IRON-ON INTERFACING: These lightweight materials used to reinforce, stabilize, and strengthen weak fabric can be helpful in repairing old tops.

IRONING BOARD OR SURFACE: A standard ironing board is generally used, but a small tabletop board is also useful. A portable, padded ironing surface is a good piece of equipment to have, especially when traveling. An extended ironing board is rectangular in shape and the same width from one end to the other. This extended board fits over your standard board, lifts off for storage, makes it easy to press large amounts of yardage, and can be purchased or made at home.

MAGIC SIZING: Made by the Faultless Starch Company and available in super-

markets. It gives body to pieces as you work. If Magic Sizing is unavailable, use spray starch.

MARKING TOOLS: These are used to mark piecing, appliqué elements, and the quilting designs. It is absolutely vital to always test the marking tool on the fabric being used. This will reveal if the tool will show on the given fabric and, most importantly, if it can be removed completely.

MASKING TAPE: This is an all-purpose tool and can be used for a myriad of tasks. Keep an average-size roll in your toolbox.

NEEDLES, HAND: These are used for all hand sewing, and they are used for finishing and detailing on machine-made quilts. Use the type and size of hand needle you find most comfortable. (The higher the number, the finer the needle.)

NEEDLES, MACHINE: Use the size needle that will work best for the type of fabric you are using, as directed by your operator's manual. The needle size should match the thread size.

NEEDLES, EMBROIDERY: Use these for embroidery work or whenever embroidery floss is used. Size #8 is the average needle.

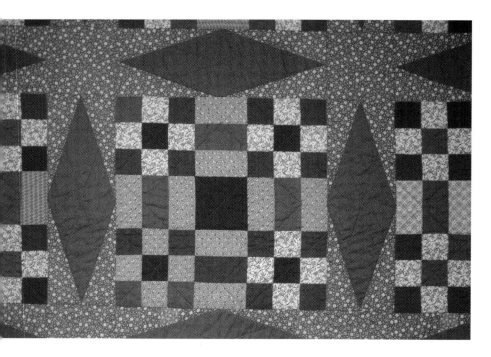

NEEDLE THREADER: Use to reduce the aggravation of threading needles, especially those with small eyes.

1/8" PAPER PUNCH: Used to punch holes in templates to mark seam allowances.

1/4" MACHINE FOOT: This piece of equipment is used for machine work to maintain a consistent 1/4" seam allowance when machine piecing.

PENCIL SHARPENER: A sharpener of any type is necessary for keeping your marking tools (except for mechanical pencils) sharp.

PERMANENT MARKING PEN: This tool can be used primarily for detailing on the quilt and for the label.

PINS: Straight pins are used to hold pieces together and are an important part of sewing any quilt by hand or machine. Choose the length and thickness you like best.

ROTARY CUTTER: Available in a range of sizes, it can cut multiple layers at one time. Always retract the blade when it's not being used.

ROTARY CUTTING MAT: A self-healing mat, used in conjunction with a rotary cutter, to protect the table surface. The mats are available in a variety of brands and sizes. Choose the one you are most comfortable working with.

ROTARY CUTTING RULER: This is a gridded, thick, acrylic (Plexiglas®) ruler, used with the rotary cutter and mat.

RULER: Use one accurate ruler for the measuring of a single project and its units.

SAFETY PIN CLOSER: A tool used to close the pins, especially when you are basting with them.

SANDPAPER: Place your fabric on fine sandpaper during the marking process.

SEAM RIPPER: Have a couple of seam rippers handy for picking seams apart or for taking out stitching when you make errors.

SEWING MACHINE: Useful for stitching and the preferred equipment for sewing for many quiltmakers. A sewing machine can be used along with hand stitching, if desired.

TEMPLATE MATERIAL: A lightweight plastic is the best choice for use in making templates.

THIMBLE: For all handwork, wear a thimble!

THREAD: Use good quality, 100% cotton thread. Color choice is personal, but it should not intrude on your work. Our preferred thread is Silk Finish cotton thread by Mettler®.

THREAD CLIPPERS: Snips or small scissors used to clip threads as you work.

UTILITY SCISSORS: Sharp, all-purpose scissors used to cut anything other than fabric.

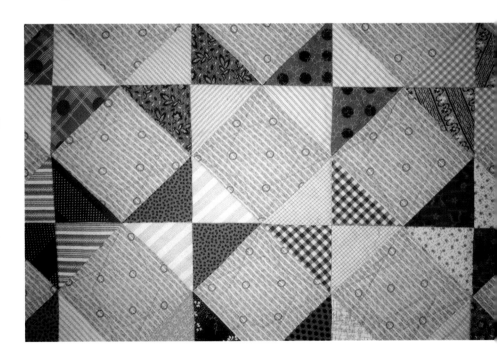

Gallery One

(Old Quilt Tops/Old Quilt Tops Completed)

The completed quilts are pictured here. Be aware that in many, in fact most, cases the completed quilt is smaller than the old top. This is because of the adjustments that were made to solve problems while completing the top. Those quilts that have added borders are larger than the old tops.

The dates given for the purchased tops are approximate. The actual dates the quilts were completed are supplied.

The more quilts and quilt tops you study carefully, the easier it will become to identify problems and how best to solve them.

Details:

Original date: 1920–1930

Completed: 1999 by
Jeannette T. Muir

Original size: 65" x 86"; completed size: 67" x 76"

Techniques: Hand pieced/machine quilted

Batting: Cotton Classic® by
Fairfield Processing
Company

Provenance: Virginia

Owner: Keith J. Quinton,
M.D.

An absolutely amazing and fantastic collection of fabrics from the 1920s and 1930s was totally overpowered by the bright purple squares and border. Even the camera could not handle the bold color. This delightful Double Pinwheel variation was another obligated purchase!

The seam allowances were adequate in width, but the width varied. Knots were used in the process, mostly backstitched, and the major intersections were triple-stitched and frequently overcast. It was a heroic effort to pick apart.

The new, all hand-pieced quilt is quasi color-coordinated. Quadriga cloth, 1940s vintage, replaces the purple center squares and border. Several additional same-vintage replacements have been used.

The quilt is named in memory of one of my very best friends, traveling companion and quilting buddy Alice Henrietta Meyer Mason (1924-1996).

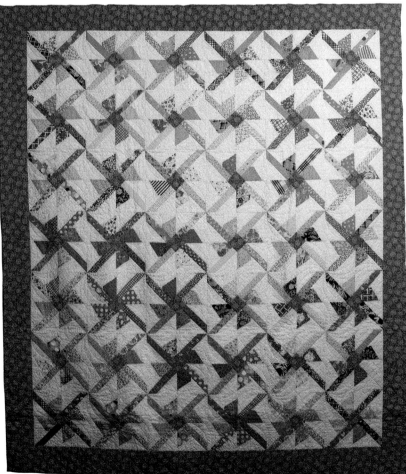

Crossed Tulips

This wonderful, "crazy," unusual top was found by Becky Herdle's son, somewhere between Austin and Dallas. One block center is not yellow like the others, but it adds to the appeal of this delightful top.

The sashing was not at all uniform, and the blocks were so badly out of shape that they had to be taken apart. The blocks were trimmed to a consistent size, sometimes cutting off portions of the patches. Four, poor-quality flannel patches were replaced. The sashing and border fabrics are new, using the same color as the original. All other fabrics are unchanged.

Details:
Original date: Circa 1940
Completed: 1997 by Becky Herdle
Original and completed size: 54" x 81"
Techniques: Hand and machine pieced/hand quilted
Batting: Polyester low loft
Provenance: Texas
Owner: Becky Herdle

Doris Mabel

Vertical rows of blocks in a staggered, undulating setting are a visual treat. Bright colors, a wide collection of prints, "mourning cloth" prints, stripes, checks, and paisleys add interest and excitement. Some heavy solids at the top and bottom appear to have been added as a last resort. Nearly all the fabrics are cotton, but some heavy rayons and wools are included.

The condition of the fabrics was good, but, as is frequently the case, no two rectangles were the same size, and it was poorly stitched. The entire top was taken apart, each piece being resized and restitched. Same-vintage fabrics, taken from sacrificial tops purchased in North Carolina, have replaced the heavy seersucker solid fabric and the very poor quality white-ground paisley.

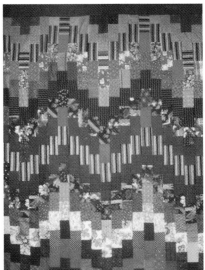

Details:
Original date: Circa 1900
Completed: 1999 by Jeannette T. Muir
Original size: 68" x 82"; completed size: 57" x 72"
Techniques: Machine pieced/machine quilted
Batting: Cotton Classic by Fairfield Processing Corporation
Provenance: Unknown, but purchased in Massachusetts
Owner: Jeannette T. Muir

Fanny May

This Bow Tie top certainly did not justify the price I paid for it, but it was a delight and made me laugh. The zigzag, "strippie" setting, the wide variety of plaids going in all directions, stains, and un-dyed white streaks in the pink print all added to the appeal.

Seams were inadequate and varied in width. All pieces were inconsistent in size and, of course, all the outside edges were on the bias. Because it was machine pieced with silk thread and long stitches, it was extremely easy to take apart.

All elements were recut, re-marked, and reassembled. The navy, plaid half-blocks at the top and bottom of the top have been replaced with 1940s fabric. The added, pieced inner border is manu-factured from an old apron that once belonged to my Aunt Hazel. The outer border is new 1940s fabric.

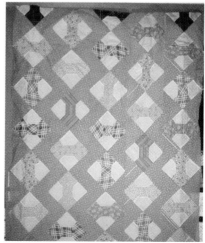

Details:
Original date: 1930s–1940s
Completed: 1995 by Jeannette T. Muir
Original size: 57" x 74"; completed size: 65" x 81"
Techniques: Machine pieced/machine quilted
Batting: Cotton Classic by Fairfield Processing Corporation
Provenance: Unknown, but purchased in Massachusetts
Owner: Jeannette T. Muir

Feedsack Fiesta

This quilt has to bring a smile to the viewer—or some other kind of reaction, at the very least! It is certainly colorful and entertaining. The entire piece, even the solid orange and green rectangles/bricks, is made of feed sacks. Whether or not these are home-dyed is unknown.

The piece was in fairly good condition, requiring the replacement of only three frayed bricks at the edge. The seam allowances flip-flopped and were stitched down in varying directions that precluded stitching in the ditch to complete the quilt. It was hand tied with white crochet cotton. Full-sized, bleached feed sacks were used for the backing. Simply controlling the crookedness and irregular measurements of this piece was a struggle, especially the double French binding process.

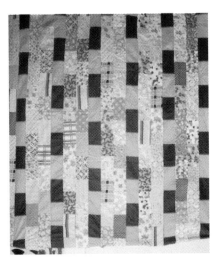

Details:
Original date: Circa 1930
Completed: 2000 by Madge Ziegler
Original size and completed size: 67.5" x 80.5"
Techniques: Machine pieced/hand tied
Batting: Warm and Natural by Warm Company
Provenance: Probably eastern Pennsylvania
Owner: Madge Ziegler

Floral Emanations

Nine "Redwork" blocks, apparently all made by the same hand, were purchased as a group. Embroidery on quilts has been used throughout history, but turkey red, commercially stamped blocks were tremendously popular from the 1920s to the 1940s.

To finish the quilt, the blocks were cut to a consistent size and set together with a same-vintage red fabric.

Details:
Original date: 1920-1940
Completed: 2000 by Patricia J. Morris
Original size: Blocks approximately 7" square
Completed quilt size: 32" x 32"
Techniques: Embroidered/machine pieced/machine quilted/hand tied
Batting: Mountain Mist, 100% cotton
Provenance: Unknown
Owner: Patricia J. Morris

Gwendolyn Julie

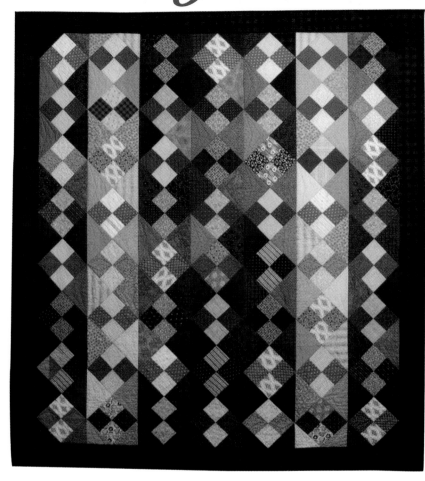

Some quilts have long been favorites for many quiltmakers, and this top is a good example. It contained a wonderful, large collection of predominantly blue, all-cotton prints from the turn of the 20th century. Note the deliberate mistake, the pink and green triangles, at the left corner. To honor the intent of the original maker, the same "error" has been incorporated into the new quilt.

The one hundred ten original four-patch blocks had been set in an uninspired arrangement without excitement or contrast placement. Very little attention was paid to grain line or consistent square size. In fact, there was not a true square in the entire lot. Bill Morris expertly disassembled the top.

Reconstruction of the top included remarking each piece to a consistent size. To maintain the scrap look, twenty-two new, year 2000 fabrics have been used as filler triangles and for the border. The new "strippie style" setting is more exciting—proof that the old fabrics and contemporary ones can be combined successfully. A few same-vintage fabrics have replaced damaged parts.

Details:
Original date: 1890-1910
Completed: 2000 by Jeannette T. Muir
Original size: *70" x 77"*; completed size: *70" x 78"*
Techniques: Machine pieced/machine quilted
Batting: Cotton Classic by Fairfield Processing
  Corporation
Provenance: Unknown
Owner: Patricia J. Morris

Kathlyn Jane

This one-patch (hexagon) top was purchased from a street vendor in Paducah, Kentucky. I was questioning the wisdom of this acquisition until, as I was laboriously picking it apart, I realized each piece was different. I had a real "charm quilt" on my hands, containing 380 pieces!

The "charm quilt" was very popular between 1860 and 1900, even more prevalent than the "crazy quilt." Ladies were just as fashion conscious as we are today. Hundreds of pinks and browns were available, as well as other colors. The "charm" lies in the fact that no two pieces are alike.

It was in fairly good condition, although quite dirty and smelly. It did survive a bath. Many of the brown fabrics were brittle and unusable, as is the case with most browns of the late 1800s.

The restoration process was lengthy, but in the long run it was the most satisfying (for Jeannette) of any project in this book. Each piece was carefully picked apart, inspected, recut, remarked, and restitched by hand. Many of the brittle brown fabrics have been stabilized with a lightweight, knit, iron-on interfacing—sometimes only the seam allowance and sometimes the entire shape. Several same-vintage replacements have been taken from sacrificial tops.

A new, diagonal setting highlights each color, so that each fabric can be compared to its neighbor while providing exciting visual contrast.

Details:
Original date: 1875-1895
Completed: 2000 by
   Jeannette T. Muir
Original size: 52" x 72";
   completed size:
   67" x 82"
Techniques: Hand
   pieced/machine
   quilted
Batting: Cotton Classic
   by Fairfield
Provenance: Joplin, Mo.
Owner: Catherine
   Koshland

 *Lillias*

Charming and understated describes the 1930s pastel, floral-pieced Wedding Ring variation, perhaps in need of some pizzazz.

The fabric was all new and in reasonably good condition, although the quality of the border was inconsistent with the better fabric in the pieced portion of the top. The seam allowances varied from 1/8" to 1/2", and the complexity of the approximately 16" blocks was clearly beyond the ability of the maker. It was pieced with long machine stitches and consequently was quite simple to take apart.

All elements were taken apart—the block was redrafted; pieces were remarked and restitched. A new 6" border, incorporating the original border fabric, was designed to create a more interesting piece. Muslin from ten-year-old curtains was used for the narrow and wide borders, as well as in the new pieced border.

Details:
Original date: 1930s
Completed: 2000 by
　　Jeannette T. Muir
Original size: 74" x 74";
　　completed size: 69" x 69"
Techniques: Machine
　　pieced/machine quilted
Batting: Cotton Classic by
　　Fairfield
Provenance: Virginia
Owner: Lillias H. Anderson

Originally intended as a summer spread, the edges of this twenty-segment Dresden Plate were finished with a wide, gold, cotton sateen facing that matched the plate centers. The seams joining the blocks were left unfinished. It was to be a simple project!

Upon closer inspection, however, the true condition of this spread was revealed. Serious stains, of an unknown substance, caused deterioration and holes. The plate centers were turned under and appliquéd to the fabric that had been placed beneath—an awkward, lumpy method.

Restoration turned out to be a tedious, complex process, including the manufacture of three new blocks to replace the damaged areas, utilizing fabric trimmed from behind the plates. New circles were cut and appliquéd on top of the inside edges of the plates. Quilting, more like wrestling, was a staggering challenge due to the size of the quilt and the complexity of the design chosen. But the result was extremely satisfying and worthwhile.

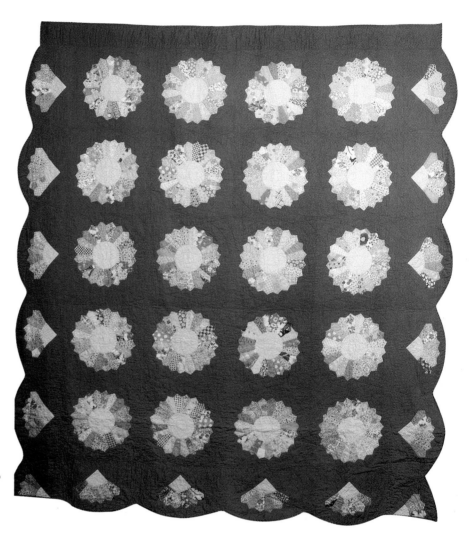

Details:
Original date: Circa 1940
Completed: 2000 by
    Jeannette T. Muir
Original and completed
    size: 89" x 100"
Techniques: Hand
    appliqué/machine
    pieced/machine quilted
Batting: Warm and White
    by Warm Company
Provenance: Virginia
Owner: Jeannette T. Muir

Lottie

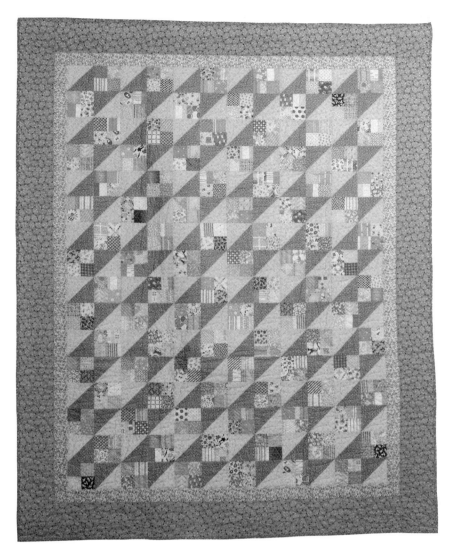

A wonderful, wide variety of 1920s to 1930s prints was totally obscured by an unusable, brittle, bleached muslin. The original Bow Tie block was abandoned in favor of a Jacob's Ladder variation, simply because it was faster and easier to assemble.

Yellow and green 1990s reproduction fabric is used for the half squares. New blue is used for the final border. Softer, less densely woven, near or same-vintage fabric would have been more desirable, but it would have been cost prohibitive even if it could have been found. A near-vintage fabric is used for the inner border.

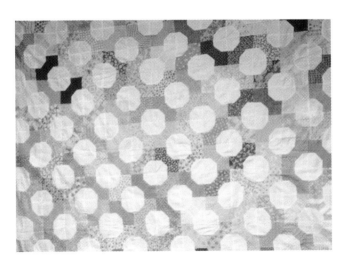

Details:
Original date: 1920s to 1930s
Completed: 1993 by Jeannette T. Muir
Original size: Unrecorded; completed size:
   47.5" x 60"
Techniques: Machine pieced/machine quilted
Batting: Cotton Classic by Fairfield Processing
   Corporation
Provenance: Unknown
Owner: Jeannette T. Muir

Maude Isabel

Twenty-five Mountain Homespun blocks take a back seat to the spectacular pieced sashing which ties the blocks together and makes this quilt a visual treat. Both in color and design, the original top was unlike any other that Jeannette had ever purchased.

The red and green fabrics were in reasonably good condition, but the pale blue print was almost like cheesecloth in quality. Many different shades of green were used, and only the side borders remained. Seam allowances were skimpy to say the least, especially at the points in the sashing.

Although not the most difficult, *Maude Isabel* takes the cake for needing the most extensive restoration. All elements were taken apart, resized, remarked, and restitched. New 1940s light fabric replaces the squares; new 1960s blue replaces the rectangles; and several of the red triangles have pieced inserts from the 1970s fabric, used wrong side up. The top and bottom borders are of new, near-vintage fabric.

The quilting process was another wrestling match because of the complex design, but it helped to cover up a multitude of pieced pieces and finally brought some life and character to the quilt.

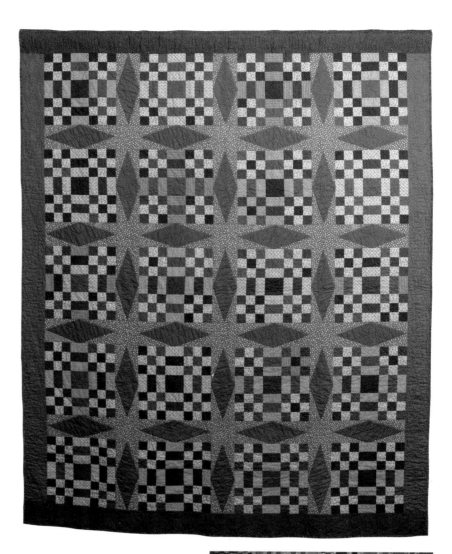

Details:
Original date: Circa 1930
Completed: 2000 by
  Jeannette T. Muir
Original size: 72" x 82";
  completed size: 66" x 80"
Techniques: Machine
  pieced/machine quilted
Batting: Cotton Classic by
  Fairfield Processing
  Corporation
Provenance: Southwest Ohio
Owner: Jeannette T. Muir

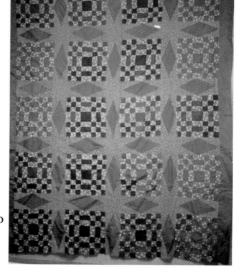

Patsy Jean

What a delight this top is! Seventy-two pinwheel blocks, on point, a huge variety of scrap fabrics, absolutely no attention paid to grain placement, and all combined in a very whimsical way. Almost certainly, because so many of the fabrics were identical, *Patsy Jean* was made by the same maker as *Vida* in *Worth Doing Twice*.

It was a delightful "disaster." All elements were totally inconsistent in size and, although most of the fabric was in good condition, some replacements were necessary. Seam allowances varied from adequate to nearly nothing. It was hand and machine stitched <u>and</u> hand basted in many areas. All the alternating plain blocks were larger than the pieced blocks, causing puckering.

Diagonal line and contrast was added by placing the cool colors in one direction and warm colors crossing in the opposite direction. Secondary, eight-pointed stars emerge and create a pleasing whole.

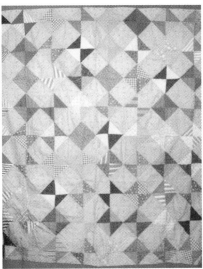

Details:
Original date: 1880-1900
Completed: 2000 by
   Jeannette T. Muir
Original size: *75" x 82"*;
   completed size: 65" x 71.5"
Techniques: Machine pieced/machine quilted
Batting: Cotton Classic by Fairfield
   Processing Corporation
Provenance: Unknown
Owner: Catherine Koshland

Sarah

The great-granddaughter of the original maker has lovingly renovated this bright, cheerful, and extraordinary Eight Pointed Star variation. The border is masterfully appliquéd with embroidered details. Nearly all of the fabric is cotton, but some leaves are silk. The top was documented by the Heritage Quilt Project of New Jersey, and appears in *New Jersey Quilts 1777 to 1950: Contributions to an American Tradition.*

The condition of the top was fair, but very fragile in some areas, especially in the yellow, pieced blocks. New, vintage, yellow fabric, used wrong side up, has been painstakingly applied throughout the entire center portion. A lightweight, knit, fusible interfacing has been used to stabilize some fabric and prevent further deterioration. Large stained areas have been over-appliquéd with near-vintage muslin. This has been an incredible, satisfying, and successful undertaking.

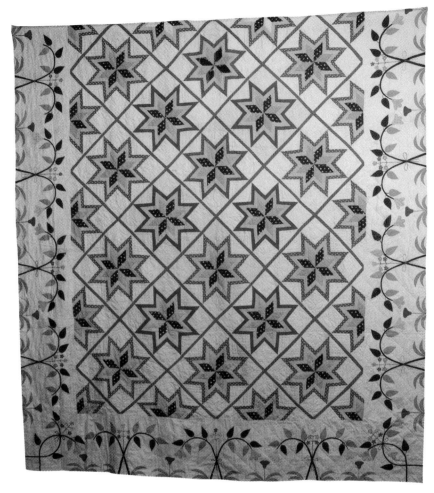

Details:

Original maker: Sarah Moore
    Kinne (1843-1878)
Original date: Circa 1860-1870
Completed: 2000 by Anita
    Claire Baker Ringen
Original and completed size:
    86" x 93.5"
Techniques: Hand pieced,
    appliquéd, embroidered,
    and quilted
Batting: Quilter's Dream
Provenance: Ferndale, New
    York (Sullivan County)
Owner: Anita Claire Baker
    Ringen

Spools

What is most interesting about this top is that we know who actually made it and where. The pattern has no special name, but the color combination is a universal favorite of quilt makers and quilt users alike.

The top did not lie flat, but was quilted without change. During the process, many seams were released and restitched, so they would lie somewhat flat.

Details:
Original maker: Edna Norman Kauffman (1889-1921)
Original date: Circa 1912
Completed: 1995 by Becky Herdle
Original and completed size: 76" x 84"
Techniques: Hand pieced/hand quilted
Batting: Polyester low loft
Provenance: Ontario, Ohio
Owner: Becky Herdle

8 Picking

(Methods, Tools)

When the pieces of a top must be picked apart to correct any of a variety of problems, this must be done very carefully or additional problems may be encountered in the process. Use a seam ripper for picking. Jeannette prefers a Clover or a Bernina® seam ripper, while Pat prefers a brass seam ripper from Heritage Crafts.

Some of the seams may not be sewn with a straight line of stitches because—just like today's quiltmakers—past stitchers had their own version of fast techniques. One of their speed methods was to eyeball the seam allowance and, for the most part, the resulting seams were by guess and by golly, not straight.

If you are removing handwork, sometimes the stitches pull out very easily while at other times hand stitching is harder to remove than machine stitching. Some hand stitching displays intermittent backstitches, while other seams might be completely backstitched.

For seams that go from one end to the other without backstitches, simply clip every eight to ten stitches and re-

move these small sections as you go, or wait until the whole seam is clipped and then take out the threads. When working on a seam that has intermittent backstitches, clip the backstitches and pull out the sections of thread lying between them. If the entire seam is backstitched, clip about every six to eight stitches and remove them one at a time, working from the

stopping point of the seam to the starting point. We've found it easy to remove seams sewn with silk thread.

When stitches in a seam are clipped with a seam ripper, the ripper can also be used to pull out sections of stitching. You may, however, prefer to just clip the stitches and to do the pulling out with a stiletto— the type most often used for embroidery work. In addition, the eye end of a needle can be used to remove the stitches. The point of a needle should not be used to remove stitches, because it can catch the fabric and distort the seam. If at all possible, do not clip and remove stitches with a scissors; it's too easy to cut into the fabric. If you must use a scissors, use a small embroidery scissors, not a big pair of fabric shears. Occasionally you work to remove a seam that has been both hand and machine stitched on the same line. This requires an extra dollop of patience.

When removing machine stitches, clip the bobbin thread—it's a little looser and easier to get at—every four or five stitches, and lift off the top thread. Sometimes machine stitches are so tiny and tight they are difficult to remove. If the color of the stitches makes them hard to see, this increases the difficulty in removing them. If you are working to remove a particularly difficult row of machine stitches, you might want to try opening up the stitched pieces—you'll be looking at the right sides of the stitched fabric—clipping every few stitches and removing the sewing thread.

If the seam allowance is inadequate, the fabric quality poor, or if the stitches present too much trouble to pick out, cut along the edge of the seams and discard the stitching and the seam allowances. This will reduce the size of the individual piece and the overall size of the old top, but sometimes it is the only solution.

When your patience—just like your fabric—is frayed, flawed, or presenting many different problems, you may need to go for brute force to pull the pieces apart. Brute force isn't advised, but if you must use it, use it carefully!

When you have the old top apart in various pieces or in sections, or if you've decided that you just want to add borders (sashing, or whatever), you are ready to make the quilt by remaking the top.

Each piece should be sprayed on both sides with Magic Sizing or, lacking that, with spray starch. Accurate templates for each piece should be made. Make sure the templates are of a size to allow for 1/4" seam allowances all around. Mark each piece with the appropriate template or marking tool, and do any necessary trimming.

Before stitching the pieces together, determine the layout you want to use for the top, as this could affect the sewing order. This layout can be exactly the same as the original top, or it can have a different arrangement of pieces. A different arrangement can be used for any number or reasons: 1) Too many pieces had to be discarded because they had holes, were torn, or had other defects. 2) You wish to make a better arrangement of blocks or a more effective balance of color. 3) You just like a new layout of your own better than the original set. 4) Another reason strikes your fancy.

You may also wish to add alternate plain blocks to a top that was originally block-to-block, or you may want to remove alternate plain blocks and make the top block-to-block. As another alternative, consider setting the blocks on point and adding triangles (ears) to the four sides to return the top to a square or a rectangular configuration. You may wish to add sashing to the original set, to remove sashing, or to change the size of it.

When experimenting with various layouts, put the possibilities (one at a time) on your pin-up wall. Study and discard any layout you don't like until you settle on the best set.

If your workspace doesn't allow for a pin-up wall, use the floor instead, standing tall to get a good perspective. (Keep pets and children, including rambunctious teenagers, out of the room until you're done.)

As you begin to piece or appliqué, you can choose to sew any given top by hand, by machine, or by a combination of the two. (English piecing, however, is sewn by hand in virtually all cases.)

For hand sewing, use the type and size of needle you find most comfortable. We prefer either a quilting #10 or a sharps #10 for hand stitching. The needle should be relatively easy to thread (try a needle threader if you are having a problem), and it should move easily though the fabric. Start and end the line of stitching with a knot, taking a backstitch every fifth stitch. You may prefer to begin and end the line of sewing with a backstitch—Jeannette uses a backstitch and Pat uses a knot.

For machine stitching, use the type and size needle that best suits the fabric you're using, and follow the recommendations in the instruction manual for your machine. A needle threader can also be used for machine needles, if your machine doesn't have an automatic threader or if the needle is difficult to thread. Start and stop with a few backstitches.

For easy, straight seam piecing, it's possible to sew from raw edge to raw edge. For other patterns, especially those with set-in pieces, don't stitch in the seam allowances. As you are stitching keep your iron handy, so you can frequently press stitched areas as you go. If you have any choice in the matter—given the pattern—press the seam allowances under the darker fabric. Do press carefully, so you don't distort the fabric. Placing a terry cloth towel under the fabric will help prevent distortion.

No matter which sewing method is used, pick your thread color with care. When hand sewing a lighter fabric to a darker fabric, use a color of thread that matches the darker fabric—one that doesn't call attention to itself. If the stitching is being done by machine, use a neutral colored thread—beige, gray, medium blue—that is in a shade that blends in with the fabric and is unobtrusive.

It is important to keep in mind that the sewing thread you should use—especially on old fabrics—is 100% cotton. Incidentally, we also use 100% cotton on new fabrics, with rare exceptions.

Once you finish sewing, press the entire top. Again, the pressing should be gentle, so you cause no harm to the top, either visually or physically.

Borders, Backing, Batting, and Sandwiching

10

Once the central portion of the top is finished and has been pressed, it's time to decide on borders. Did the original top, as purchased, have a border as the first consideration? If it did, and you've removed it, do you want to replace it with the original border fabric or a different fabric? Do you want to leave the border off? Or, if it never had a border, do you want to add one? All of these are possibilities, and, in large part, they depend on personal preference. Usually both of us prefer to border our quilts, old and new. We feel it finishes the quilt, especially for traditional or old quilts, visually

holding and containing the central part. Without a border, the top is likely to seem unfinished, as though it's going to fall off the edge. Borders also help control bias edges, which are common in old tops.

If you decide to replace or add a border, be certain the work is as technically accurate as possible and that the fabric, be it old or new, is of good quality. These same caveats also should be observed for the backing, the binding, and the batting.

For example, let's say you've decided to go with borders of old or new fabric and you want the border to be 3" wide. Don't just cut the fabric 3" wide by "x" miles long and start sewing it to the top at one end, sewing it to the other end, and cutting off the excess. This almost ensures a rippled border. The correct way is to measure the top from one end to the other down the center, and from one edge to the other across the center. These numbers,

plus the extra inches for meeting and for seam allowances, are the size to cut. In most cases, adding the width of the border to each end of the border pieces will give you the extra amount needed for meeting.

A determination also has to be made as to the manner of meeting: borders can be mitered or they can meet squarely. In the latter case, the border should be sewn from top to bottom on each side and then from one end of the border to the other end on the top and bottom. Just before you start to sew on each piece of the border, pin it carefully to the finished top at short intervals, easing where necessary. Once the entire top is bordered, it should be thoroughly and carefully pressed.

We hear a lot these days about "backart." Basically, "backart" thematically extends the quilt top. It also allows the quilt to be reversible, and it is entirely appropriate for contemporary and innovative work. But it seems out of sync with the old traditional work.

For the backing, you can use vintage fabric but, because of its general unavailability and other reasons (loosely woven, narrow width, high price, lack of strength to support the quilting in many cases), it is probably a good idea to go with new fabric (availability, width, affordability, strength enough to stabilize the entire top and to support the quilting). When using a new fabric, choose one in a color that is compatible with the colors in the top. Of course, muslin (of good quality) can always be used on traditional or old quilts. It may not be the most exciting fabric to use on the back, but it is entirely appropriate. Be sure to wash, dry, and press the quilt backing.

Rarely will you be using fabric wide enough for the backing, unless you are working on a wall hanging. It is a matter of personal choice to use extra wide material as quilt backing. We do not find this an entirely satisfactory option, preferring to use the standard 45" wide fabric, even though it will have to be seamed. The grain of the fabric should run vertically down the back to stabilize the quilt and prevent stretching, especially if the completed quilt is to be used as a wall hanging. We advise you to avoid a seam down the center of the back. It is better to have a full width of fabric down the cen-ter of the back and a half (to a full width) on either side of it.

Remove the selvages and stitch the lengths together using a 1/2" seam allowance, which is then pressed open. Be sure to make the backing about two inches bigger on each side of the top.

You need to consider several things in choosing your batting: Are you hand or machine quilting the piece, what loft do you want, what is the fiber content, is the batting a good quality brand, and which is easiest for you to work with—your personal, subjective choice.

Jeannette does the majority of her quilting by machine and prefers (almost exclusively) to use Cotton Classic by Fairfield Processing Corporation, which is a blend of 80% cotton and 20% polyester. Pat does some machine quilting and for that prefers Mountain Mist cotton. For hand quilting, Pat prefers Thermore® by Hobbs Bonded Fibers or Mountain Mist Quilt Lite®. All of these are quite low loft battings. If the batting you're using requires preparation, follow the manufacturer's directions. Cut the batting 1" bigger on each side of the top.

At this point, you are ready to sandwich the three layers and baste them together. The chosen quilting design can be marked before or after the basting step. Press the backing for a final time and, using masking tape, tape it down— right side of the fabric down, wrong side of the fabric up. Tape it smoothly, evenly, squarely, and flat on a large surface. The surface easiest to use is a floor (tiled, linoleum, wood, etc.). Large tables pushed together can be used, or it's even possible to work on a low-pile carpet. Center the batting on the backing, being sure it's flat and even. With care, do a final pressing of the top and center it on the batting.

Then, working from the center out, baste the three layers of the fabric together. The basting can be done with thread or safety pins. That is a personal choice. If thread basting, it's important to use white, cotton thread. For safety pin basting, use size #1 non-rusting safety pins. Be most careful not to create bubbles and pleats during the basting but to end up with the basted quilt smooth and flat. The last row of basting should be done around the edges.

The sandwiching and basting will go more smoothly, considerably faster, and be less tedious if you have a quilting colleague (or two or three) to help you. Remember to reward them with coffee and goodies for their help!

Quilting

(Hand, Machine, Combination)

Hand Quilting:

(From Pat's point of view) Mainly covering both old and new quilts

When we discuss quilting, we are talking about doing small, even stitches that accomplish two major tasks: Holding together the three layers of the quilt and providing an additional design element to the work. The appearance of the completed quilt is affected by the type of quilting design and by the amount of quilting. Background support quilting is important in highlighting the quilting design and in holding the three layers together securely.

Quilting designs may be found in books and magazines, purchased from dealers, or invented from your own imagination. The ease of execution of the quilting designs is tied to the degree of difficulty of the quilting, and the kinds of fabric and batting you are using. It's important that you like your chosen quilting design, or you will not enjoy quilting the work and likely will not complete it. The quilting design may be done by marking around a template, using a stencil, quilting in the ditch, stippling, or quilting along the edge of masking or bias tape.

Generally, any kind of fabric can be used in a quilt but certain fabrics require special care. For the majority of quilts, however, 100% cotton is the fabric of choice. Be sure to pre-wash any cotton fabric that you purchase. The backing, pre-washed, should not shadow through the top and should be the same type of good quality fabric used for the top. The fabric, top and back, should be pressed before being used.

The first choice in a marking tool is one that is visible while quilting and removable when the quilting is completed. Some marking tools are used before sandwiching and others after. Choose from: A regular, lead pencil of a hardness or softness you prefer; a silver artist/student pencil or one in a color that will work on that particular quilt; a soapstone

pencil; a fine edge leftover soap that has been left to thoroughly dry; powdered chalk; masking tape; ribbon; bias tape; pressure sensitive designs; chalk pencils; or simply eyeball where the quilting will go. Whatever marking tool you use, be certain to keep it sharp. Remember to mark lightly. While there are other tools (water soluble pens, pencils, and the like), we will not use them because of their chemical content.

When quilting, you can work on a frame (of any shape), work in a hoop, or work in your hands. Pat's preference is working in a hoop.

Regular sewing thread is used to construct the top and for quilting. Carefully consider the color thread you'll use for both steps. Use a single thread, a maximum of 18" long, for hand quilting.

"Betweens" needles are usually used for quilting, but "sharps" can also be used. It's the choice of the quilter. The lower the number of the hand needle, the bigger the needle; the higher the number of the hand needle, the finer the needle.

The first step in the quilting process is to start a line of quilting. You have to be sure that both the starting and ending of a line of quilting is not obvious—no backstitches for starting and ending. The best method to start and end the quilting is with a knot. Bury the knot in the batting layer after it is tied, and then

pop the knot through the top, burying the excess thread in the batting layer. Be sure to have at least 3" of thread left to comfortably knot the end of the line of quilting.

It's important to work at getting the quilting stitches, both front and back, even in size. This will only be mastered with practice. Once you manage to get the stitches even, you can work on getting them smaller.

The quilting stitch is done by inserting the needle straight down into the quilt sandwich, going through all three layers, and moving the needle forward. The needle is then immediately tipped sharply upward and out the top. More than one stitch may be put on the needle at one time. Put as many stitches on the needle as is comfortable for you to pull through the sandwich with ease. This is called "rocking the needle" or a "rocker" stitch. Pat prefers to put only one stitch on the needle at a time. This may seem to take more time than putting multiple stitches on, but if you build up a smooth quilting rhythm, the speed of your stitching will build up.

Quilt from the center out. This will give you better control than quilting from side to side or end to end. While quilting, be certain to wear a thimble on your pushing finger. This will help you get better control of the stitches

and protect your finger from stabbing, bleeding, and pain.

Care should be taken to make sure that the stitches are pulled tightly enough to hold the three layers securely together. They should not just lie loosely on the top of the quilt. Conversely, the stitches shouldn't be pulled so tightly that they form bubbles or gathers that would distort the quilt.

Once the quilting is completed, take out the basting. Remove the basting stitches one at a time from the outside to the center, the opposite of how they were put in.

Quilting truly makes the quilt, be it done by hand or machine. It brings the quilt to life and gives it a practical or decorative life of it own. It is the most important part of the quilt. No quilting, no quilt.

Machine Quilting:

(From Jeannette's point of view) Mainly covering old quilts

Quilting gives personality and character to the quilt. It adds texture and dimension, enhances the design, and discourages wrinkling, as well as providing protection for the precious fabrics. A completed quilt will last much longer than an uncompleted top.

Basically, there are two methods of machine quilting. The first is machine-guided—using a regular machine with an attachment called a walking foot. This is Jeannette's method of choice and where her expertise lies. Other terms for the walking foot attachment are "plaid matcher"

or "even-feed" foot. The other method is called free-motion. It is accomplished by lowering the feed dogs and using, or not using, attachments. More and more quilters are quilting by machine.

Long-arm/commercial machine quilting is gaining recognition, but the most proficient operators are usually booked in advance, and (depending on the intricacy of the quilting design, the material being used, and the expertise and experience of the quilter) the work will take a shorter or longer amount of time. They are professionals who have worked very hard to perfect their skills. Choose wisely by asking to see samples of their work, the patterns and designs they use, what they offer and for how much. Satisfied customers are

the best endorsement.

There are many excellent books available on the subject of machine quilting, some of which are listed in the bibliography.

When working on an old top, it would be wonderful and exciting to have fabric of the same vintage for the backing as for the top, but it would be very cost prohibitive even if you could find a sufficient quantity. However, a more densely woven fabric will add protection to the top as well as provide a more stable base for the quilting stitches. Color and design, of course, are a personal preference, but if you need to hide many beginnings and endings, choose a busy print.

The manufacturers have listened to our requests for flatter batts, specifically for

machine quilting. Different companies make a wide variety of brands. Some of the batts are cotton, some are polyester, while still others are blends, some of which may need preparation before quilting. Follow the manufacturer's instructions. A cotton batt is generally the choice for old quilts and for machine quilting. Unfold the batt and allow it to relax. The batt should be washed without agitation. This also removes any salts or chemicals that remain. The batt can be machine dried, making it more uniform in thickness while removing creases.

Extra pinning (2-3" apart) is needed when basting. The vintage fabric is frequently loosely woven and on the bias. The extra pinning will provide less stress in any one area (the bias). One-inch brass safety pins are smooth and easy to fasten and unfasten. Pins are inserted, but they are not fastened until the piece is un-taped.

When choosing a needle for quilting, sizes 75/11 or 80/12 are recommended. The quilting 75/11 and universal 80/12 needles can be used interchangeably. Just remember to use good quality, sharp needles and change them frequently.

Regular, 100% cotton thread, sewing weight, is suggested for machine quilting (e.g. Silk Finish by Mettler). If the thread breaks, it can always be replaced. The fabric cannot. Choose a color that blends in.

Sometimes choosing the right quilting pattern is the most difficult portion of the quiltmaking process, but it is also one of the most important features, necessary to create an overall pleasing and effective product. Scale drawings can be copied and used for doodling until the right solution is reached. There is no easy way, but persistence can be very rewarding. Remember, there are entire books of quilting designs.

When preparing to mark your fabric, keep in mind that vintage fabric is more frequently loosely woven than contemporary fabric, making marking more difficult. Chalk markers are very temporary and can be used only for short distances. Chalk pencils (white, pink, or blue) will provide longer lasting lines, but require very frequent sharpening, and may be difficult to remove. Always mark as lightly as possible.

Many vintage fabrics stretch, especially those loosely woven or those cut on the bias, so it is important not to distort them during the quilting process. By pushing a small "speed bump" directly in front of the needle to ease in the fabric, distortion can be avoided. Allow the feed dogs and the walking foot to work together. Do not put a drag on or spread the fabric. Push it gently. Your function is to be sure the quilt sandwich moves smoothly under the needle.

Combination Quilting

(From Pat's point of view) Covering both old and new quilts

Combination quilting is, quite simply, doing both hand and machine quilting on the same quilt. Use your instincts here.

12

Completing the Work

Your project is now quilted and your quilt is done. WRONG! Now the edges have to be finished, the final step in making the quilt. There are quite a few finishing options. But the method used most often is binding.

From time to time another edge-finishing method might be appropriate, but generally you'll find yourself binding the edges.

If you're binding the quilt, old or new, use a fabric that is of a compatible color, thread count, and vintage. The binding can be straight, cross, or bias (especially for curves), as you prefer, unless the quilt demands one or the other—our preference is cross grain. Avoid commercial bias tape in all cases. Generally, the quality is not good and the color is usually not a decent choice in relation to the quilt.

When binding, whether your quilt is made by hand or machine, the usual practice is to stitch the raw edges to the top of the quilt by machine and the folded edge of the binding to the back of the quilt by hand. In preparation for the binding process, using the walking foot, stitch around the outside of the quilt approximately 3/16" from the edge. Square up the corners and clean finish the edges using a rotary cutter, mat, and ruler.

Cut 2 1/4" strips across the width of the binding fabric to measure ten inches longer than the perimeter of the quilt. Stitch these pieces together using diagonal seams **(Figure 1)** to get the length needed. Trim these seams and press them open, then cut one end at a 45-degree angle. Fold the strip in half lengthwise, wrong sides together (right sides out) and press.

Walk the binding around the perimeter, and adjust the starting and ending points to make sure the binding is of sufficient length to avoid seams at the corners. The starting point for applying the binding should be about the middle of the bottom edge of the piece. Leave the first 5-6" of the binding unstitched—the end cut at an angle.

Working with a 1/4" seam

allowance on the top side of the quilt, match the raw edges of the binding to the raw edges of the quilt. Stitch the binding to the quilt by machine, using a walking foot. Stitch to within 1/4" of the corner, backstitch, and remove from sewing machine, clipping the threads only **(Figure 2)**. Fold the binding **(Figures 3 and 4)** and stitch to the next corner. Repeat this procedure at all corners. Leave 5" of the binding unstitched when nearing the original starting point. Pin the binding in place.

Fold up the excess binding to match the beginning 45° angle **(Figure 5)**. Crease with your thumb. Unfold and mark the inside of the crease.

Add 1/2" marking beyond the crease line. Open up the binding to a single layer of fabric, extend the 45° line, and cut. Join the ends with a 1/4" seam, matching folds **(Figure 6)**. Press this seam open. Stitch the remaining section to the quilt top.

Smooth the binding carefully to the back, and hand stitch it in place using matching-colored thread and mitering corners (top and back) as you work. Be sure to stitch the miters closed as you work on each corner. Remember to pin the binding to the quilt (as Jeannette does) or use binding clips (which Pat prefers). Be careful not to stretch either the quilt or the binding during the edge fin-

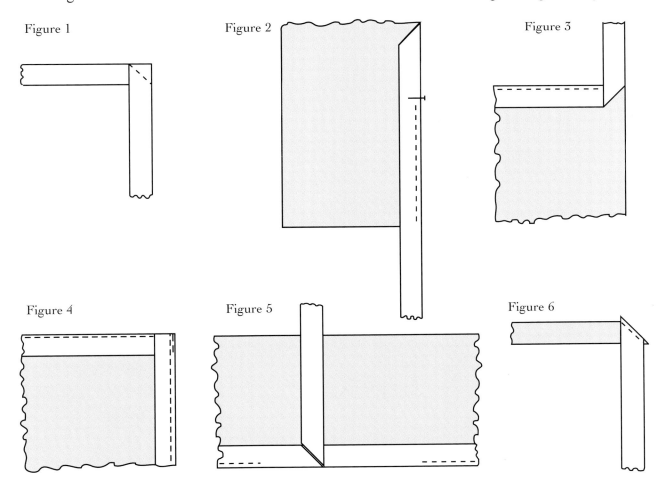

Figure 1

Figure 2

Figure 3

Figure 4

Figure 5

Figure 6

Completing the Work ❖ **47**

ishing. Don't forget that the binding should be completely filled with batting.

Once the edge finishing is completed, your quilt is done (except for a couple of details), and ready to use on a bed. If you prefer to hang your quilt on your wall, hang it in an exhibit, or enter it in competition, you will have to add a sleeve across the top of the back.

If you decide to put a sleeve on, first choose the fabric you will use for the sleeve. For this purpose, there are three fabrics, in order of preference, that will work: 1) the same fabric as was used for the backing of the quilt, 2) a fabric that has the same color and value ranges as made up the top, and 3) muslin. Prewash any fabric you will use to make the sleeve.

A 4" sleeve is generally the accepted and requested size for most quilt shows and is very workable for hanging in your home. To construct the sleeve, cut the fabric 9" long by the width of the quilt—including binding, piecing if necessary—to get the needed width. Narrowly hem the short edges. Fold this piece in half lengthwise, wrong sides together, and stitch with a 1/2" seam.

Turn the resultant tube until the seam allowances run down the center of the tube; this is now the wrong, or back, side of the sleeve. Press the sleeve thoroughly, being careful to smoothly press the seam allowances open. Place

the wrong, or back, side of the sleeve to the top back of the quilt, just below the top binding and inside the side bindings. Pin it in place. Using matching-colored thread, hand stitch the sleeve securely in place, leaving the top layer of the sleeve unstitched at the ends, and being careful not to penetrate the right side of the quilt with these stitches.

After the sleeve is added, wash your project. This washing will remove any markings (if you have not used a permanent marker), smudges, and soil.

At this point, prepare a label containing, at a minimum, the title of the piece, the name of the maker, the date, and whatever other information you deem appropriate. Stitch the label to the back of the quilt in a bottom corner. The label can be either hand or machine embroidered, computer generated, purchased, or of any other kind that strikes your fancy.

Should you wish to add embellishments to your quilt that weren't added earlier, now is the time to add them. Let the type of quilt and your imagination guide you in the use of embellishments.

Complete the documentation of your quilt by taking a photo of the finished quilt. This photo, along with the photo of the old top before any work was done on it, will provide a visual demonstration of the changes, if any, that you made. The photo documentation papers should

include the finished size, any changes you made, and any other pertinent information.

You may want to have your quilt appraised for insurance purposes or because you want to sell it. Use a reliable, quilt-knowledgeable appraiser. A list of appraisers certified by the American Quilter's Society is available from that organization. If you have your quilt appraised, make a copy of the appraisal, attach a photo, and put the original of the appraisal in a safe deposit box.

Insuring your quilt treasures is not a bad idea. If for no other reason, this will give your family some notion of what you have. Insurance can also financially reimburse any losses you might suffer, even though it can't replace the work itself.

Having reached this point, you truly have a completed quilt with all the details. You have just one thing left to do: **ENJOY THE FRUIT OF YOUR LABOR!**

(Contemporary Versions Inspired by Old Quilts)

✦ Blue Roses

By Patricia J. Morris

Luscious Leftovers

By Nancy S. Breland

Tickled Pink

By Marion Nicoll

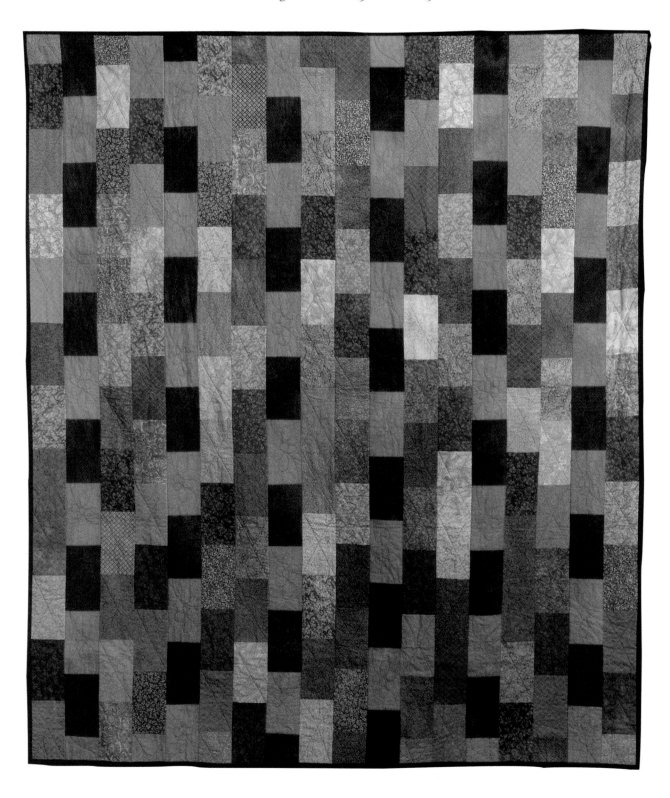

Trumpet Vine

By Madge Ziegler

Values In Blue

By Margaret Y. Bowling

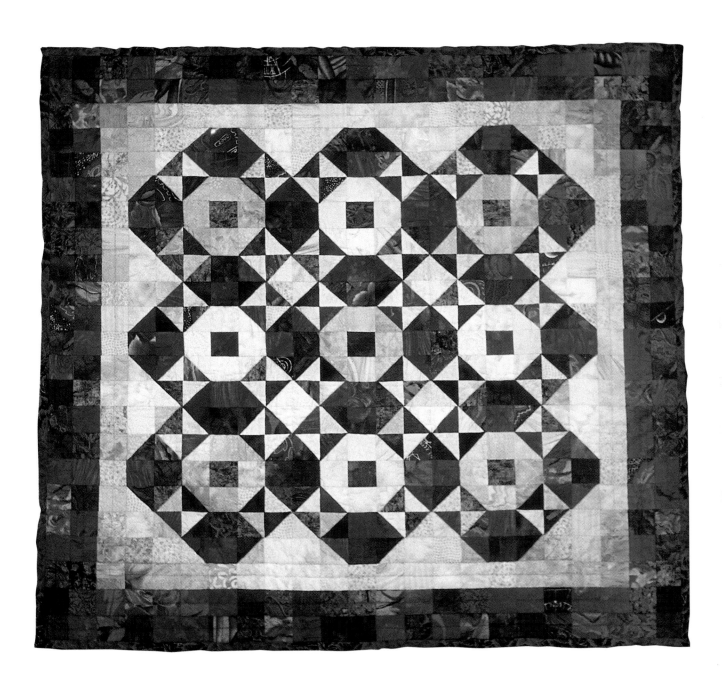

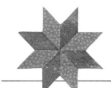

Eight O' Clock Seating

By Carolyn E. Larason

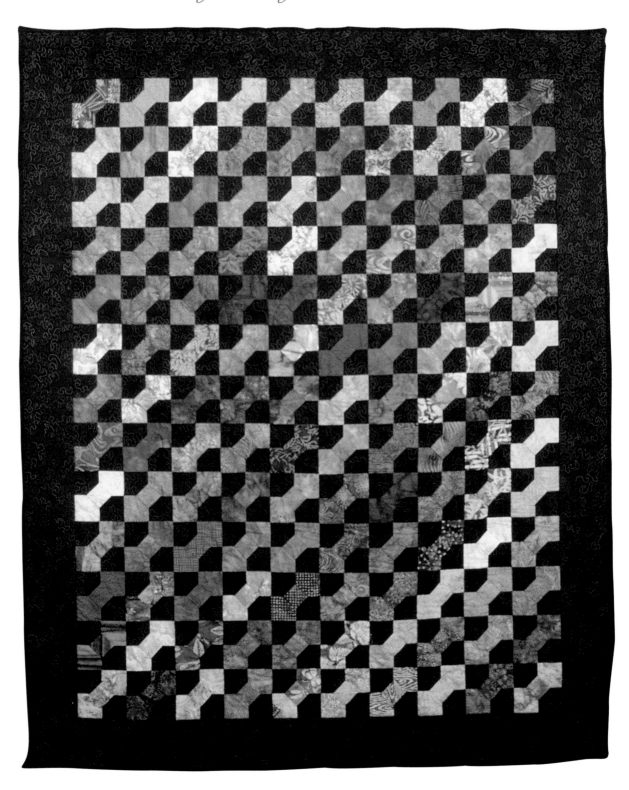

Jersey Sunflowers

By Jeannie Roulet Minchak

Poppy's Whirligigs

By Jane Hamilton

Primary Hex-Election 2000

By Lynn G. Kough

Turning Point

By Merry May

Cat Crossing

By Irene Sherman

Colorplay

By Linda A. Hall

Garden View

By Joyce Murrin

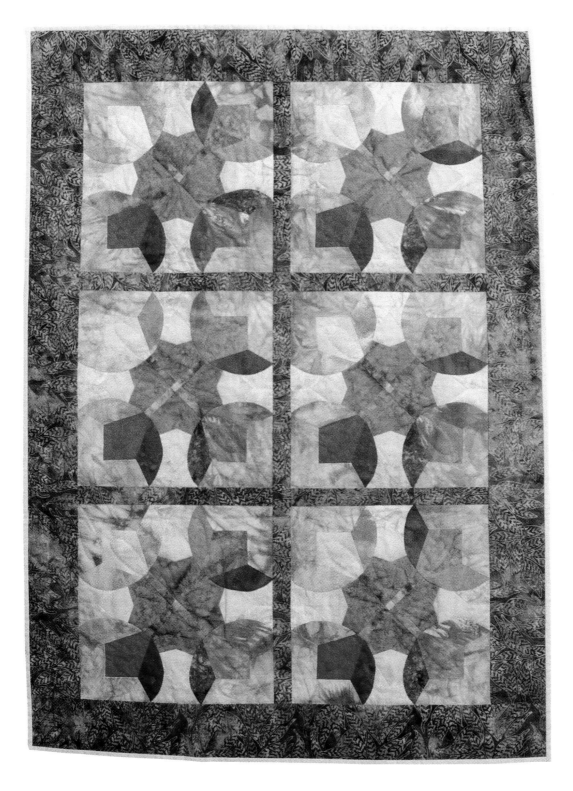

Montanafires.2000

By Mary Kay Hitchner

Sarasponda

By Judith Thompson

Projects

(Directions and Detail Photos)

General Instructions

A consistent format is used for the presentation of fifteen contemporary versions of the old quilts shown in Gallery One. The instructions begin with a brief description and close-up photo of the quilt. Refer to Gallery Two for a full photo.

The techniques involved are followed by suggested fabrics and approximate yardage requirements.

Instructions are presented to reproduce the quilts that are pictured in the new quilt gallery. Suggested levels of expertise are also included. All of the templates/patterns may be resized according to your needs. Be sure to adjust the yardage requirements, as necessary.

Precision piecing is sometimes described as the old-fashioned method of assembling patchwork. Templates are used, especially when accuracy is most important. To prepare the templates, place the template material on top of the pattern. Using a fine-point permanent pen, transfer the dots, add a 1/4" seam allowance beyond the corner dots, and cut on the outside line. Punch out the dots with a 1/8" paper punch.

When tracing the template to the wrong side of the fabric, mark the entire circle with a sharp pencil. The circles are much more visible than just a dot, especially on printed fabric. Sandpaper underneath the fabric will help to stabilize the fabric and prevent distortion. Connect the circles using the straight edge of the template. The edge is also useful for scooping up the fabric from the sandpaper.

Pin seams, right sides together, matching corresponding circles. Begin stitching the seam at one circle, and stop stitching at the other, leaving the seam allowances unstitched. If the seam is on the bias, take a backstitch every 1 1/2", and every 2 1/2" on straight of grain or cross-grain seams for added strength.

Remember ... there are no rules. Enjoy the process!!!

Blue Roses

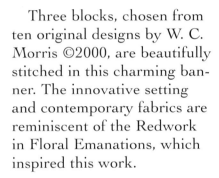

(27" x 24")
(Basic)

Patricia J. Morris ©2000
Pitman, New Jersey

Three blocks, chosen from ten original designs by W. C. Morris ©2000, are beautifully stitched in this charming banner. The innovative setting and contemporary fabrics are reminiscent of the Redwork in Floral Emanations, which inspired this work.

Techniques: Whipped back-stitch embroidery (Redwork); quilting by hand or machine; tying

Fabrics: Light, medium, and dark colored batiks or other cottons; DMC® embroidery floss

Approximate yardage:
- 1/4 yard light-colored fabric for embroidered blocks
- 1/4 yard medium-colored fabric for alternating plain block
- 1/4 yard dark-colored fabric for border

Assembly:

1. Embroidery blocks

a. Using Template A, mark and cut three 7" light-colored squares.
b. Choose three of the flower designs, and trace them on squares using a light box or window.
c. Embroider the designs using a whipped backstitch in one, two, or three strands of floss in your choice of color.

2. Setting the blocks

a. Using Template A, mark and cut one 7" medium-colored square.
b. Using Template B, mark and cut two 7" medium-colored half-square triangles.
c. Using Template C, mark and cut one medium-colored quarter-square triangle.
d. Arrange the elements and stitch them together as shown in **Figure 1**.

3. Add a 3" border.

Quilting and tying: The dotted lines in **Figure 1** represent suggested quilting tracks. The dots represent optional locations for tying.

Artist's statement: The project began when I acquired a number of Redwork blocks on muslin that had never been fashioned into a quilt. The floral design blocks were then assembled, sashed, and bordered in red cotton and finished as a wall hanging. For the new version, I elected to do just a few original floral designs in blue or purple floss on batik, alternating with a block and triangles in medium fabric. I then put these into a banner bordered with a purple print. By using blue work, the finished banner echoes the original without attempting to replicate it.

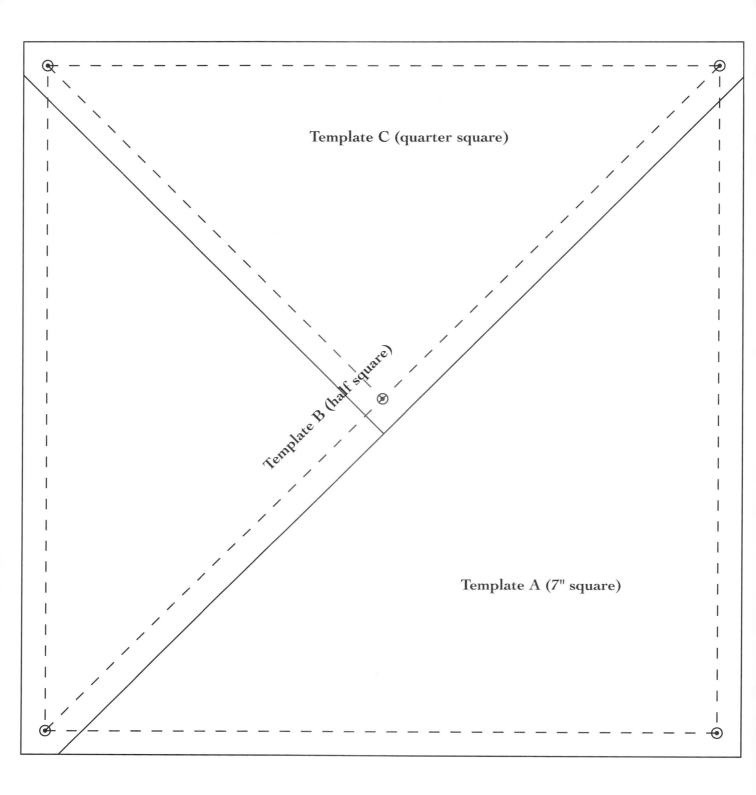

Template C (quarter square)

Template B (half square)

Template A (7" square)

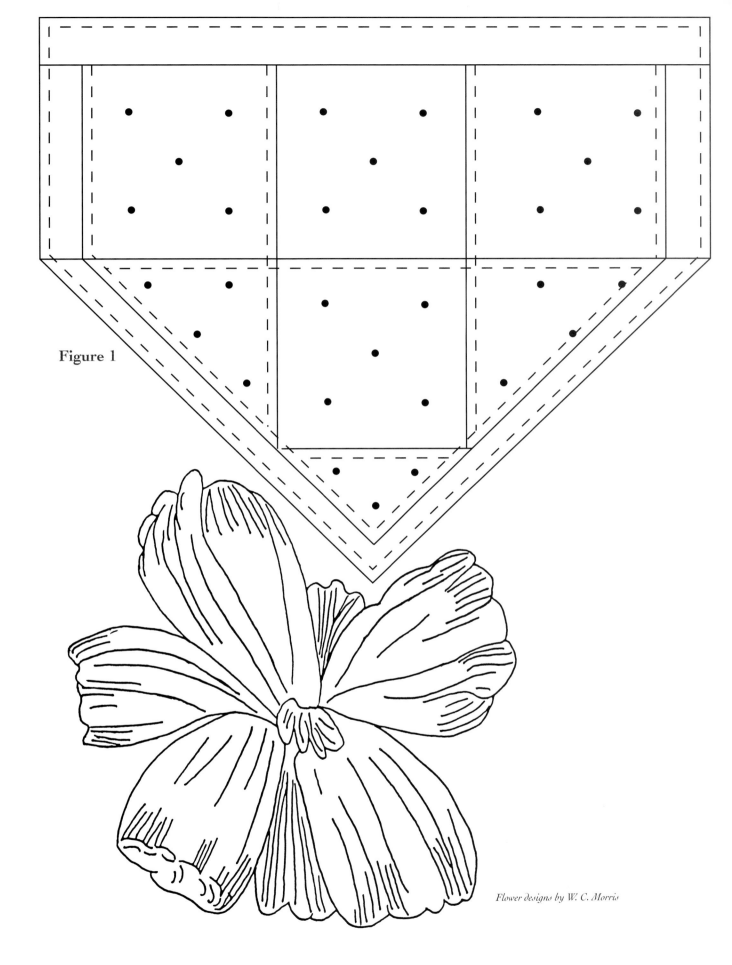

Figure 1

Flower designs by W. C. Morris

Luscious Leftovers

(43" x 43")

(Basic)

Nancy S. Breland 2000
Pennington, New Jersey

A restful palette has been chosen for this reproduction of *Gwendolyn Julie*. The hot pink accents and luminous quasi-medallion area bring it to life.

Techniques: Quick machine piecing (no templates, seam allowances are included)

Fabrics: Various scraps of batiks, in compatible colors, using a full range of values from light to dark

Approximate yardage:
- 1 1/2 yards (total) scrap fabrics
- 1/4 yard inner border
- 1/2 yard outer border
- 1/2 yard binding
- 1 1/2 yards backing (scraps optional)

Assembly:

1. Prepare sixteen nine-patch blocks, as shown in **Figure 1**. Cut 1 3/4" squares.

2. Cut at least sixty-five 4 1/4" squares.

3. On a "design wall," arrange the nine-patch blocks and squares as shown in **Figure 2**. Colored squares indicate placement of nine-patch blocks. **Note:** Extra squares will allow you to play with the arrangement until it pleases you.

4. Add a 1 1/2" inner border.

5. Add a 3 1/2" outer border.

6. Optional: Leftover squares may be used to piece the backing.

Quilting: Free-motion quilting is chosen here with the emphasis on the center medallion. Decorative threads show up well on the batik background grid, in an overall pattern.

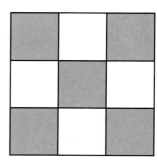

Figure 1

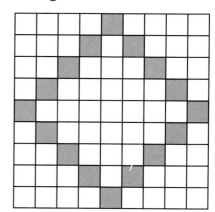

Figure 2

Tickled Pink

Inspired by *Patsy Jean*, Marion has created a wonderful mosaic using a soft, warm, monochromatic palette. Diagonal block setting and contrast create excitement and motion. Marion was tickled pink to be invited to participate in this project.

Technique: Quick machine piecing (no templates)

Fabrics: A light color "theme" fabric for the background; a medium color fabric for half of the triangles; a variety of darker/brighter colors for the remainder of the triangles; compatible fabric for the border; and fabric for backing

(59" x 64")
(Basic)

Marion Nicoll 2000
Bozeman, Montana
Quilted by Tracy Peterson Yadon

Approximate yardage:
- 1 1/2 yards of light, "theme" fabric for the background squares and outside triangles
- 1 yard medium color for half of the triangles
- 1 yard (total) darker/brighter fabrics for the remaining half of the triangles
- 2 yards for the border (this may be pieced, requiring less yardage)
- 4 yards for the backing

Cutting:
Background ("theme" fabric):
- Cut seven strips, 4 1/2" wide, into fifty-six 4 1/2" squares.
- Cut two and one half strips, 6 7/8" wide, into fourteen 6 7/8" squares; cut each square in half diagonally; then cut each triangle in half.
- Cut one 5 3/8" square; cut it in half diagonally; then cut each triangle in half.

Medium:
- Cut five strips 5 3/8" wide, into thirty-six 5 3/8" squares; cut the squares in half diagonally, then cut each tri-

angle in half. (You may need six strips, depending on the width of the fabric.)

Dark/Bright:
- Cut five strips, 5 3/8" wide, into thirty-six 5 3/8" squares; cut the squares in half diagonally, then cut each triangle in half. (You may need six strips, depending on the width of the fabric.)

Border:
- Cut a 6" border along the length of fabric to avoid piecing.

Assembly:

1. For each block, sew one medium-color triangle to one dark/bright-color triangle (**Figure 1**). Repeat. Press the seams toward the darker fabric. Sew each half together, matching center seams (**Figure 2**). Square up, if necessary, and trim to 4 1/2" square.

2. Using a design wall, place the squares "on point," alternating background squares with pieced triangle squares to create the pattern as shown in **Figure 3**.

3. Place small background triangles in corners and larger background triangles along edges.

4. Starting with an outside triangle, stitch the rows together diagonally, placing a background square between each pieced square. (**Figure 4**)

5. Following the diagram, stitch the diagonal rows together, matching points and seams, where necessary.

6. Trim the outside edge, if necessary, allowing a 1/4" seam allowance beyond the points of the triangles.

7. Add a border.

Quilting: The dotted lines in **Figure 5** represent optional quilting tracks. As an alternative, the triangle squares may be stitched in the ditch, with continuous line quilting in the solid squares, as shown.

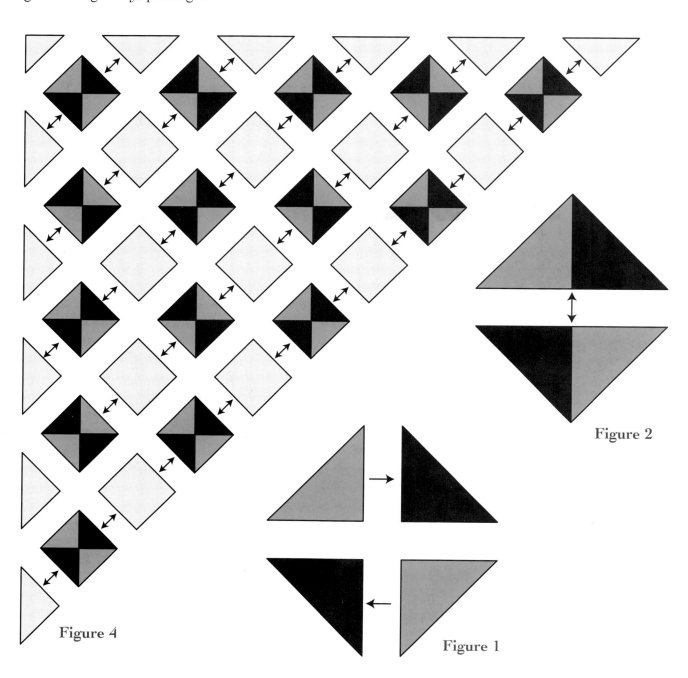

Figure 2

Figure 4

Figure 1

Figure 3

☐ Background "theme"

▨ Medium

■ Dark/Bright

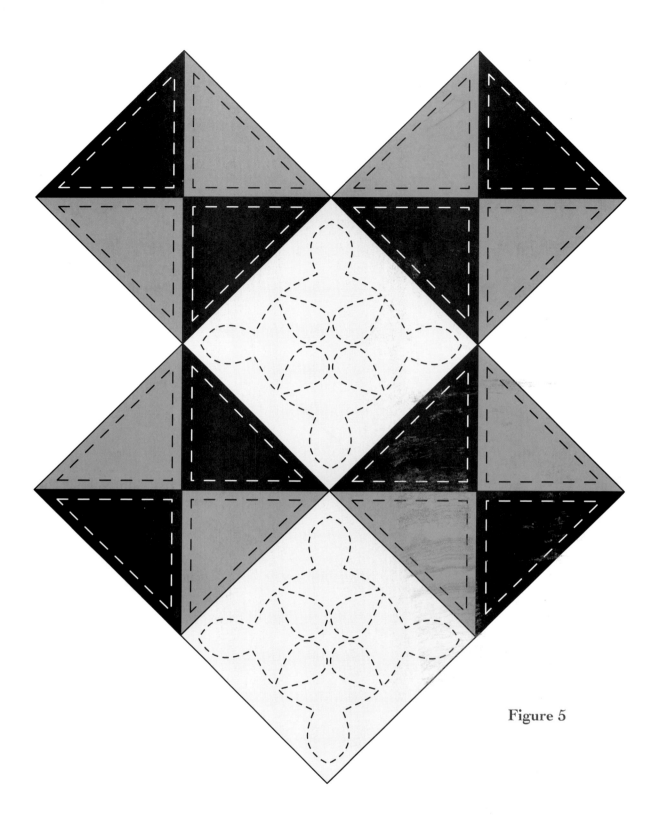

Figure 5

Trumpet Vine

(67.5" x 80.5")
(Basic)

Madge Ziegler 2000
Newark, Delaware

Rectangles of hand-dyed, solid fabrics and over-dyed, tone-on-tone, commercial printed fabrics are set in vertical rows in this contemporary version of *Feedsack Fiesta*. The size may be altered by increasing the number or length of the vertical rows or by changing the size of the rectangles.

Technique: Quick piecing by machine (no templates)

Fabrics: A wide variety of prints and two contrasting solids

Approximate yardage:
• A total of 3 1/2 yards of assorted prints

• 1 yard <u>each</u> of two contrasting solids

Assembly: (Note: rectangles are cut 4 1/4" x 7 1/2")

1. Cut 144 rectangles from assorted prints.

2. Cut 36 rectangles from <u>each</u> solid.

3. Stitch the solid rectangles into six vertical rows of twelve rectangles each, alternating colors. (Be sure to stitch the <u>short</u> edges together.)

4. Stitch the prints into twelve vertical rows of twelve rectangles each.

5. Join the rows as shown in **Figure 1**, matching the seam allowances in one row to the centers of the adjacent rectangles.

6. Excess half-rectangles at the top or bottom of the rows are easily trimmed after the rows are stitched together.

Quilting: Stitch in the "ditches" adjacent to the vertical seams. Optional, machine-guided tracks in the print fabric rectangles are indicated by the dotted lines in **Figure 2**. Connecting free-motion designs are used in the solid rows, flowers on the orange fabric, and leaves on the green fabric, as indicated in **Figure 3** and **Figure 4**.

Artist's statement: The new version is exactly the same size as the old top. The idea of recycling, embodied in the making of quilts with feed-sack fabrics, was continued by recycling the printed fabrics from my stash. They were over-dyed to change their appearance and help them coordinate within the quilt top. Large pieces of printed fabrics from my stash were over-dyed for the back of the quilt. I managed to make use of fabrics that would have stayed on the shelf forever. I tried to dye the two solids to match the orange and green in the old top. I didn't want to stray too far from the stark design and colors of the old top, which is what attracted me in the first place.

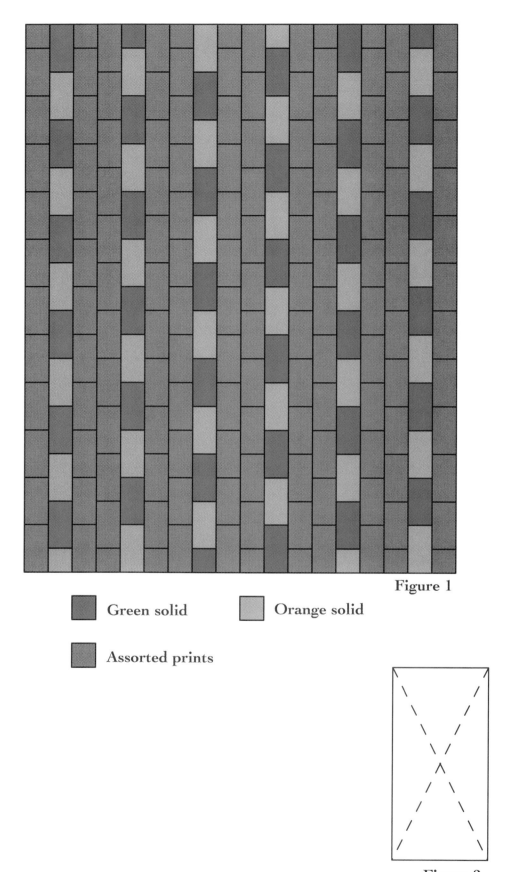

Figure 1

Green solid   Orange solid

Assorted prints

Figure 2

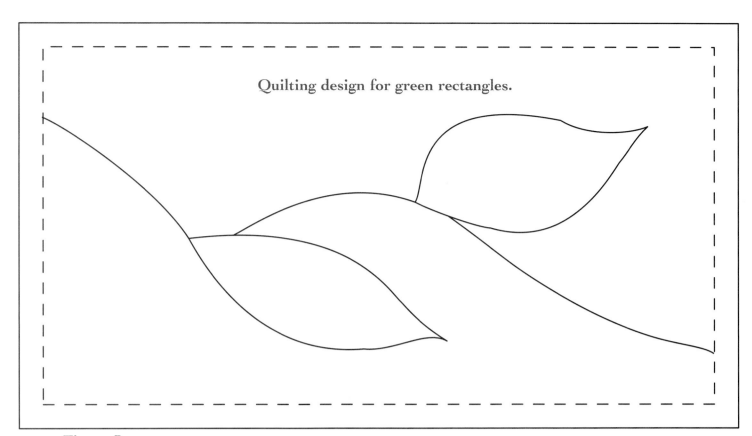

Quilting design for green rectangles.

Figure 3

Quilting design for orange rectangles.

Figure 4

Values in Blue

(34 1/2" x 34 1/2")
(Basic)

Margaret Y. Bowling 2000
Elkview, West Virginia

A simple reversal of light and dark fabrics, using jewel-toned colors, dramatically alters the appearance of the old quilt, *Lillias*. Fifty scrap fabrics in the blue-green palette have been used here, creating a cool, crisp wall hanging.

Techniques: Quick piecing by machine, machine quilting

Fabrics: A wide variety of light and dark scrap fabrics

Approximate yardage:
- A total of sixty-four 2" light squares, and fifty-seven 2" dark squares
- A total of eighty-four 3" light squares, and eighty-four 3" dark squares
- For borders, cut seventy-two 2" light squares, and 168 of the 2" dark squares

Assembly:

1. Place a light 3" square over a dark 3" square, right sides together. Draw a diagonal line.

2. Stitch a 1/4" seam on each side of the diagonal line.

3. Cut on the drawn line.

4. Press the seam toward the dark fabric, and trim to a 2" square.

5. Repeat with the remaining 3" squares.

6. Audition all the squares on a design wall as shown in **Figure 1**.

7. The borders are made entirely of squares, one light and two dark.

Note: Some fabrics work well on both sides. Experiment.

Quilting: Most of the quilting tracks are in the ditch. The squares in the borders are quilted in long lines in the centers of the squares.

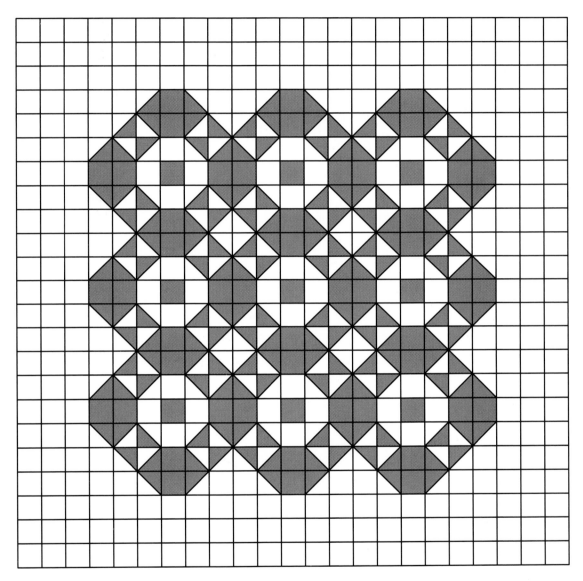

Figure 1

Eight O' Clock Seating

(60" x 75")

(Intermediate)

Carolyn E. Larason 2000
Williamstown, New Jersey

Diagonal color bands create a spectacular visual treat in this contemporary re-make of the traditional Bow Tie pattern in *Fanny May*. The "stipple" quilting, using variegated thread, adds stunning and beautiful texture.

Techniques: Quick machine piecing (no templates), and folding

Fabrics: A wide variety of batik scraps on a black background

Approximate yardage:
- 3 yards (total) of batik scrap fabric
- 3 1/2 yards black cotton for background, borders, and binding
- 4 1/2 yards for backing

Cutting:
- For each Bow Tie, cut three 3" squares of the same fabric. You will need 130 sets, for a total of 390, 3" squares.
- Cut background fabric as follows:
- Eight 2 1/2" strips by width of fabric for binding
- Two 5 1/2" x 67" lengths for side borders
- Two 5 1/2" x 63" lengths for top and bottom borders
- 260 squares measuring 3" (Slightly longer than needed. Trim later to fit.)

Assembly:

1. For each Bow Tie block use three squares of the same batik and two background squares.

2. Fold one batik square in

half, <u>wrong</u> sides together, to form a rectangle.

3. Place one batik square and one background square <u>right</u> sides together with the rectangle between. Align the raw edges and sew a 1/4" seam, encasing one end of the rectangle. (**Figure 1**)

4. Finger-press the seam away from the rectangle.

5. Place the remaining batik square and background square <u>right</u> sides together, encasing the other end of the rectangle, reversing positions of the fabrics. (**Figure 2**)

6. Sew a 1/4" seam, and finger press the seam away from the rectangle.

7. Matching raw edges and seams that have been finger pressed in opposite directions (**Figure 3**), sew a 1/4" seam across the top edge.

8. Open the block and press flat. (**Figure 4**)

9. Repeat the process, making a total of 130 blocks.

10. Arrange the blocks on a design board as desired. Stitch in thirteen rows of ten blocks each.

11. Add 5" finished borders, cut to the exact measurement of the top.

Quilting: "Stipple" quilt all background areas and borders by machine.

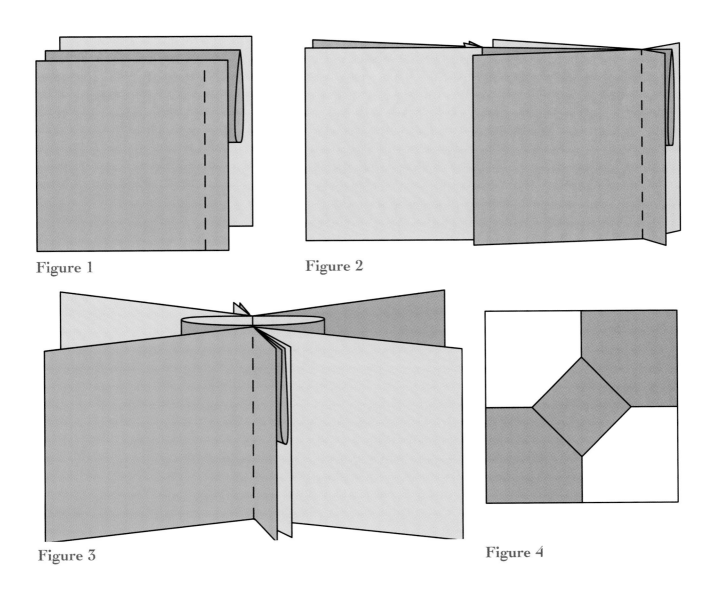

Figure 1

Figure 2

Figure 3

Figure 4

Jersey Sunflowers

(69" x 69")

(Intermediate)

**Jeannie Roulet Minchak 2000
Moorestown, New Jersey**

A dazzling assortment of batik-style fabrics creates a stunning contemporary version of *Lois Margaret*. The swirling quilting designs create texture and motion. Notice the perfectly executed binding, prepared from 2 1/2" pieces of the wide variety of fabrics.

Techniques: Appliqué and piecing by hand or machine

Fabrics: A wide variety of hand-dyes and batiks

Approximate yardage:
- At least twenty, light to medium colored "fat quarters" or 1/4 yard cuts
- 1 yard medium colored fabric for flower centers and inner border
- 5 1/2 yards dark fabric for background

Assembly:

1. Using Template A, cut 268 petals of the light to medium colored fabric. (Cut 14 from each fabric, giving you a few more than you actually need.)

2. Fold each petal, right sides together, and stitch a 1/4" seam, as shown in **Figure 1**. Trim the corner and press as shown in **Figure 2**.

3. Stitch twenty petals together to form each sunflower, stitching from the top of the petal towards the center. Prepare nine complete sunflowers.

4. Cut nine 16 1/2" x 16 1/2" background squares.

5. Appliqué one sunflower to each square, by hand or machine.

6. Using Template B, trace and cut nine centers. Be sure to add seam allowances. Prepare edges using your preferred method.

7. Appliqué over centers of each sunflower.

8. Join completed blocks in rows of three by three.

9. Add a 1" (finished) inner border, and a 9" (finished) outer border.

10. Prepare four corner sunflowers by stitching ten petals together. Appliqué the sunflowers to the corners of the border.

11. Using half of Template B (add seam allowance) mark, cut, and prepare the appliqué. Apply the appliqué to the centers of the corner sunflowers.

12. Prepare eight border sunflowers by stitching six petals together. Appliqué the sunflowers to the outside borders.

13. Using one quarter of Template B (add seam allowance) mark, cut, and prepare the appliqué, and apply it to the centers of the border sunflowers.

Quilting: Stitch in the "ditch" around each sunflower and every other petal. See **Figure 4** for an optional pattern of free-motion swirls and wind (inspired by Lee Cleland's *Quilting Makes the Quilt*). Random swirls are used in the sunflower centers. An adaptation of a traditional pattern from the 1930s (Quilting Template), may be used between the inside sunflowers and along the inside edge.

Artist's Statement: Several years ago, my husband's company transferred him from Maine to New Jersey. In two months time, I felt I had lost my home, my friends, my quilting life, and my garden. I came to learn that I lost very little, and I added friends and a whole new quilting life. *Jersey Sunflowers* is a reminder that my garden grows wherever I do.

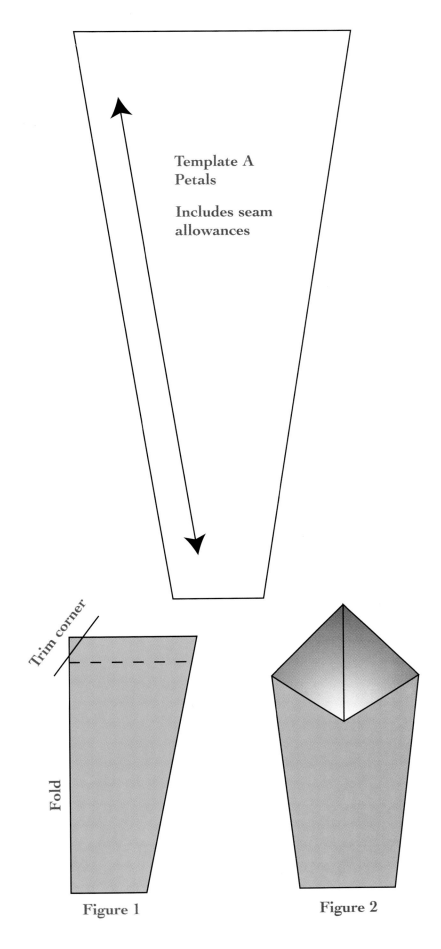

Template A
Petals

Includes seam allowances

Trim corner

Fold

Figure 1

Figure 2

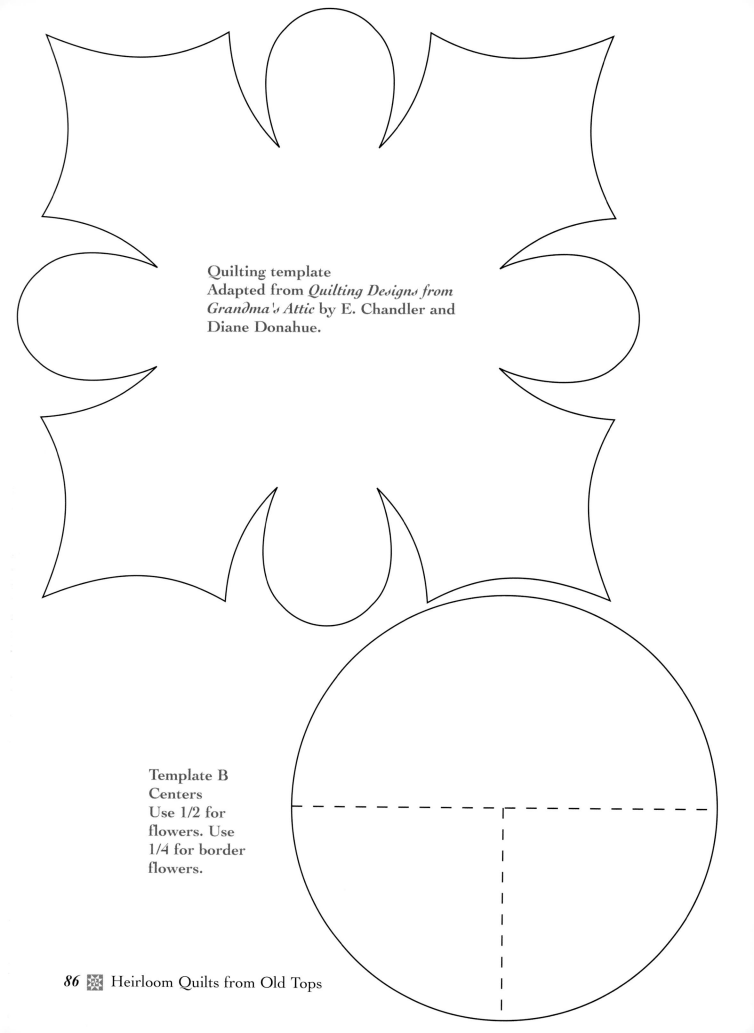

Quilting template
Adapted from *Quilting Designs from Grandma's Attic* by E. Chandler and Diane Donahue.

Template B
Centers
Use 1/2 for
flowers. Use
1/4 for border
flowers.

Figure 3

Poppy's Whirligigs

(54" x 72")

(Intermediate)

Jane Hamilton 2000
Kennett Square, Pennsylvania

Thirty-two "Flying Pin-wheel" blocks, as inspired by the blocks in *Alice Henrietta*, surround the center medallion. The rainbow palette, lively printed fabrics, and a successful combination of blocks, make this a very cheerful quilt.

Techniques: Quick piecing, precision piecing by hand or machine, and machine quilting

Fabrics: A wide variety of bright, rainbow-colored prints; white solid; and white on white

Approximate yardage:
- 3 1/4 yards white background
- 1/4 yard white on white (center background)
- A wide variety of "fat quarters" in rainbow colors

Assembly:

1. For <u>each</u> of the four quick-pieced, medallion, center blocks (**Figure 1**), cut four 3 7/8" orange print fabric squares; two 3 7/8" white-on-white background squares; two 3 7/8" yellow print squares; and one 3 1/2" yellow square.

a. Quick piece half-square triangles by placing one orange square and one background square, right sides together. Draw a diagonal line.

b. Stitch 1/4" seam on each side of the diagonal line.

c. Cut on the drawn line. (Each square yields two half-square triangles.)

d. Repeat steps a, b, and c.

e. Repeat procedure, placing remaining orange squares and yellow squares, right sides together.

f. Place the blocks on a design wall or set them aside.

2. For each of the eight pinwheel variation blocks (**Figure 2**) that surround the center, cut four 3 7/8" pink squares; four 3 7/8" white squares; and one 3 1/2" red square. Quick piece as described in Step 1.

3. For each of the four blocks at the corners of the medallion center (**Figure 3**), cut one 4" orange square; four 1 3/4" x 4" yellow rectangles; four 1 3/4" x 4" green rectangles; one 5 1/4" white square; and two 3 3/4" white squares.

a. Cut the 5 1/4" square diagonally in both directions.

b. Stitch the rectangles together, lengthwise, right sides together.

c. Stitch the triangles to the rectangles, as shown in **Figure 4**. Background triangles' points will extend beyond the edge.

d. Cut 3 3/4" background squares in half, diagonally.

e. Assemble block as shown in **Figure 5**. Numbers indicate the piecing sequence.

f. Trim the points. Pieces will "float" away from the seam.

4. The remaining 32 "whirligig" blocks are precision pieced, using Templates A through E. Be sure to transfer construction circles "a" for matching in piecing sequence.

a. **Figure 6** represents 1/4 of the block.

b. Piece as shown in **Figure 7**. Numbers indicate the piecing sequence.

c. **Figure 8** represents a full block.

5. Stitch together two rows of six "whirligig" blocks for the top, two rows of six "whirligig" blocks for the bottom, and a row of four for each side.

Quilting: Machine "stipple" quilt all background areas. Quilt remaining areas as desired.

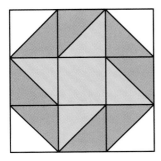

Figure 1

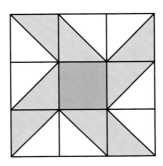

Figure 2

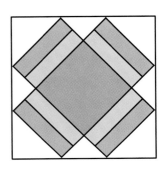

Figure 3

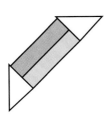

Figure 4

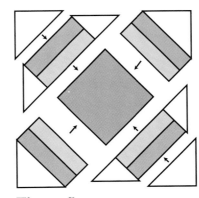

Figure 5

Figure 6

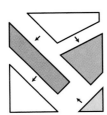

Figure 7

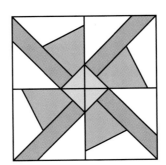

Figure 8

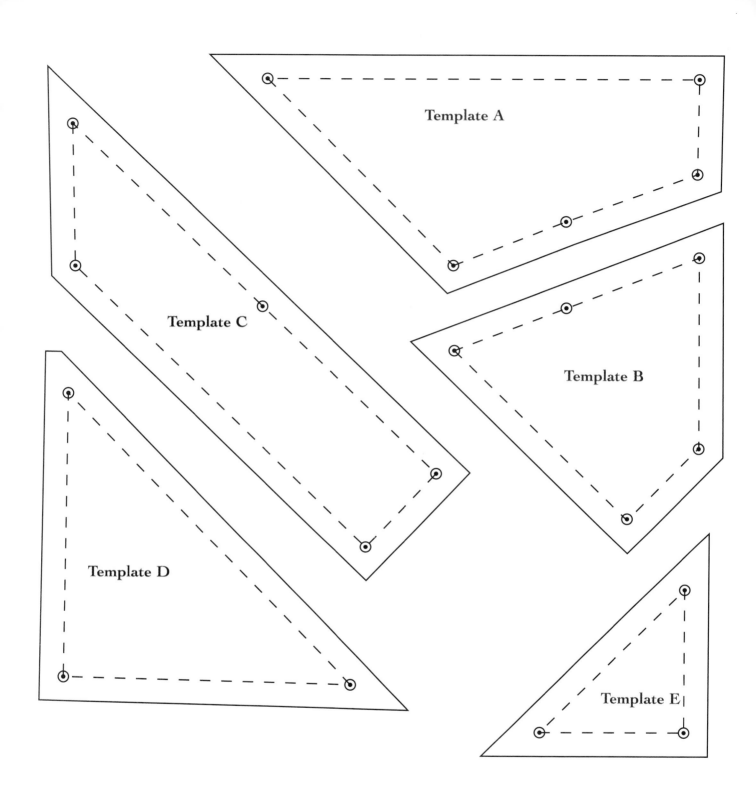

Template A

Template C

Template B

Template D

Template E

Primary Hex— Election 2000

(38" x 56")

(Intermediate)

Lynn G. Kough ©2000
Chandler, Arizona

The contemporary version of *Kathlyn Jane* adds a three-dimensional quality as well as diagonal motion and excitement. The vibrant colors make a bold statement.

Techniques: Precision piecing by hand or machine

Fabrics: Assorted reds, yellows, and blues (seven each); assorted beige/browns (six each); russet browns for setting triangles, border and binding

Approximate yardage:
• 1/8 yard <u>each</u> seven reds, yellows, and blues
• 1/8 yard <u>each</u> six light, medium, and dark browns
• 1 1/2 yards russet brown for setting triangles, border, and binding

Assembly:

1. Using Template A, cut forty-eight half-hexagons each from red, yellow, blue, light brown, medium brown, and dark brown fabrics.

2. Arrange the pieces on a design wall as shown in **Figure 1**. Shading indicates the placement of blue half-hexagons.

Suggestion: Design diagonally.

3. Half-hexagons are stitched in groups of three. (**Figure 2** or **Figure 3**)

4. These triangles are joined in vertical strips. Prepare six strips and stitch them together to make the top.

5. Using Template B, cut nineteen setting triangles.

6. Set in small triangles at the top and bottom of the pieced center. **Note**: Trim bottom corner triangles after insertion.

7. Add 4" borders, or personal preference.

Quilting: Stitch in the ditch along all diagonal seams, as well as adjacent to the border. Two parallel lines, 1/2" apart, finish the border.

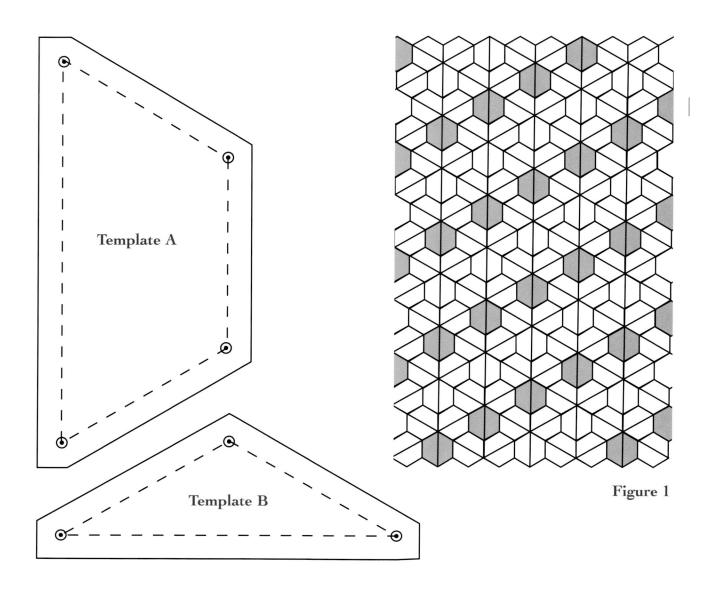

Template A

Template B

Figure 1

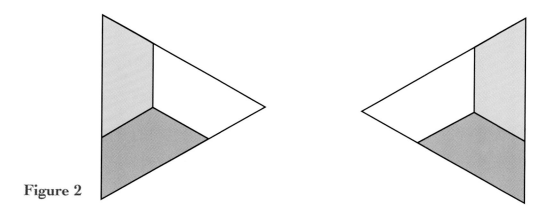

Figure 2

Figure 3

Turning Point

(38" x 38")
(Intermediate)

Merry May 2000
Tuckahoe, New Jersey

From the original quilt, *Lottie*, I reinterpreted its initial one-block repeat into two slightly different blocks. Both blocks use exactly the same basic units (two four-patches and two half-square triangles), but you can see just one of the many possible layout options these two blocks can offer.

Technique: Piecing by hand or machine

Fabrics: A variety of light, medium, and dark hand-dyed fabrics. Some are solids; others are multi-colored with a lot of visual texture. A single, multi-colored, light fabric was used in all of the half-square triangle units. It was repeated here and there in the four-patch units as well.

Approximate yardage:
- 1/4 yard of several light fabrics
- 1/4 yard of several medium fabrics
- 1/4 yard of several dark fabrics
- Additional 1/2 yard of dark fabric for inner border and binding
- 1/2 yard for outer border

Assembly: (Note: "Innie" and "Outie" refer to the placement of the point of the large triangles in each block.)

1. For each "Outie" block (**Figure 1**), mark and cut four light and four medium squares using Template A. Also cut two light (background) and two dark half-triangles using Template B. Make a total of thirteen "Outie" blocks.

2. For each "Innie" block (**Figure 2**), mark and cut four medium and four dark squares using Template A. Also cut two light (background) and two dark half-triangles using Template B. Make a total of twelve "Innie" blocks.

3. Assemble each block as indicated in **Figure 3** and **Figure 4**.

4. Alternate the "Outie" and "Innie" blocks; refer to full gallery photo for suggested design arrangement.

5. Cut four 1 1/2"-wide strips of dark fabric for the inner border. Add them to the center section.

6. Cut four 3 1/2"-wide strips of outer border fabric, and add them to the previous section.

Quilting: Machine-guided, straight tracks highlight the darker diagonal lines, and stitching in the ditch provides texture and dimension in the background squares. A graceful continuous-line swag motif adds motion and interest to the border.

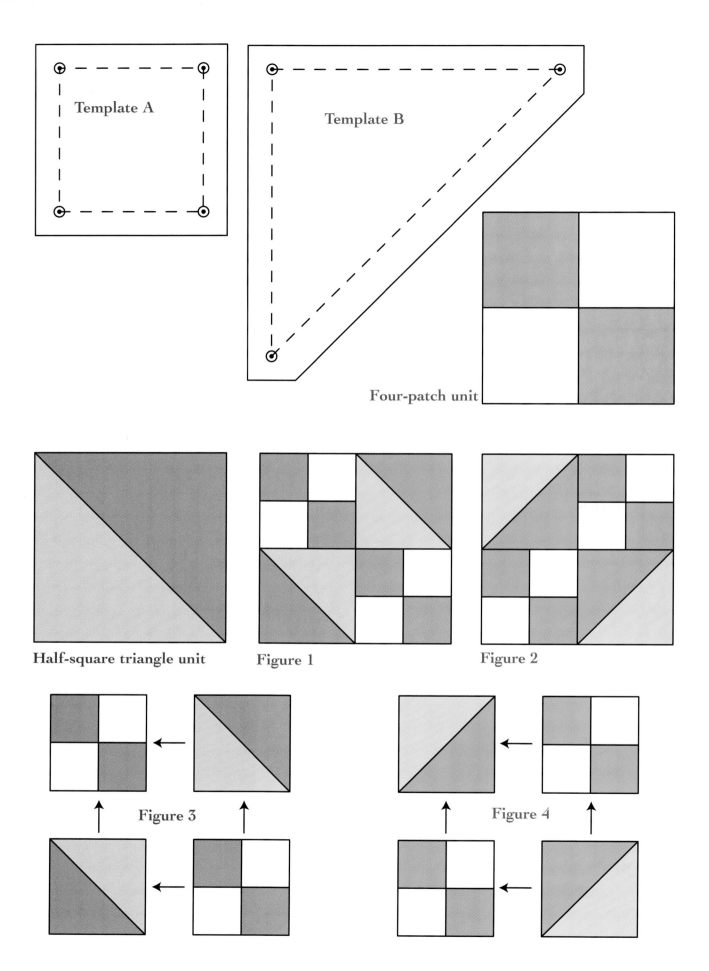

Template A

Template B

Four-patch unit

Half-square triangle unit

Figure 1

Figure 2

Figure 3

Figure 4

Cat Crossing

(30" x 30")
(Advanced)

Irene Sherman, ©2000
Scranton, Pennsylvania

The narrow, patterned, stripe-theme fabric appears to weave over and under the star points in the sashing of this small piece inspired by *Maude Isabel*. Five of the squares (posts) have been "fussy cut" into four pieces to continue the theme and to create interest.

Technique: Precision piecing by hand or machine using templates

Fabrics: Solid colors coordinating with the printed theme fabric

Approximate yardage:
- 288 linear inches theme fabric
- 2/3 yard muslin
- 1/2 yard gold solid
- 3/4 yard rust solid
- 3/4 yard black solid

Assembly:

1. For each unit (**Figure 1**), mark and cut seven muslin squares and six gold squares using Template A and two gold triangles using Template K.

2. Assemble the unit in checkerboard style.

3. For each unit (**Figure 2**), mark and cut one rust triangle using Template B, and one black triangle using Template C.

4. Stitch the triangles together, and join them to unit one (**Figure 1**).

5. Mark and cut one theme fabric piece using Template D.

6. For each unit (**Figure 3**), mark and cut one rust triangle using Template B <u>reversed</u>, one theme fabric piece using Template E, one rust piece using Template G, one black piece using Template F, and one muslin piece using Template J.

7. Stitch the segments together, as indicated in **Figure 3**.

8. Join the segments to the theme fabric, piece D (Template D).

9. Mark and cut one black triangle using Template H.

10. Assemble all units together as indicated by arrows.

11. Prepare thirty-six complete units (**Figure 4**).

12. To duplicate "fussy cut" sashing squares (posts), mark and cut four identical squares from the theme fabric using Template M.

13. Assemble the squares, matching small "a" corners as shown in **Figure 5**.

Block construction: Prepare nine full blocks as follows:
1. Matching "x" of one unit (**Figure 4**) to "x" in large square (L), or "fussy cut" square, stitch seam only about 1 1/2", as indicated by the dotted line in **Figure 6**, leaving remainder unstitched.

2. Continue stitching in clockwise direction around the center square. Numbers indicate piecing sequence, the last seam (5) completing the block.

3. To complete the top, join all nine blocks together.

Quilting: The dotted lines in **Figure 4** indicate optional quilting tracks. Additional tracks may be quilted in the ditch adjacent to the theme fabric and the star points.

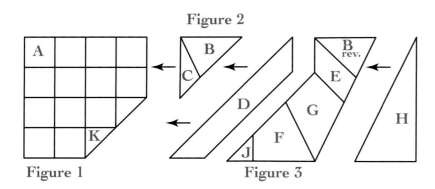

Figure 2

Figure 1

Figure 3

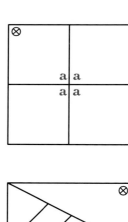

Figure 5

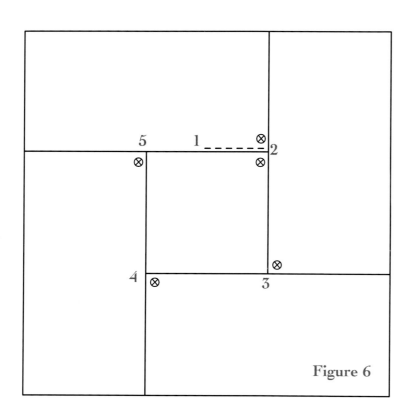

Figure 6

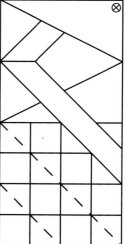

Figure 4

Colorplay

(54" x 54")

(Advanced)

Linda A. Hall ©2000
Douglassville, Pennsylvania

Inspired by *Spools*, *Colorplay* is a scrap quilt—a great way to rediscover your "stash" and play with what you already have. Of course, you may need to purchase additional fabric to fill in the blanks with colors and values that may be missing, but that is called "augmenting your inventory."

Technique: Piecing by hand or machine

Fabrics: A rainbow palette of all 100% cotton prints has been used here, with gradations of gray to black

Approximate yardage:
• A wide variety of scrap fabrics in light, medium, and dark values, from 1/8 yard to 3/8 yard, depending on usage
• 1 3/4 yards for the outer border (This may be pieced, requiring less yardage.)

Assembly: To duplicate *Colorplay*, refer to full gallery photo for suggested fabric placement. Use **Figure 1** to color in your own palette.

Suggestion: In order to piece the blocks successfully, take a piece of 8 1/2" x 11" white paper and cut a window in it the size of one row of blocks (5/8" x 6 1/4"). Place the window over the first row of the design and assemble the pieces for that row only.

1. For each block (**Figure 2**), mark and cut four pieces using Template A and four pieces using Template B.

2. Stitch units A to units B as shown in **Figure 3**. Press seams toward the triangles.

3. Stitch the quarters into halves. Press the seam toward the left, on the wrong side.

4. Join the two halves. The center seams should automatically be distributed in opposite directions.

5. Clip the center back in the seam allowance and press all

seams, "fanning" clockwise to eliminate bulk in the center.

6. Join blocks together, two at a time, until the first row is assembled. Check your diagram to make sure the colors are in the right order.

7. Press all block-joining seams in one direction. The next row will be pressed in the opposite direction.

Suggestion: Place each completed row on a design wall.

8. Slide the window down to cover the next row and proceed as before.

9. Continue until all ten rows are assembled.

10. Stand back to "audition" the rows. Make any changes now, before stitching the rows together.

11. Stitch the rows together by twos, then fours, until the top is assembled.

12. Add a 3" border, or personal preference.

Quilting: Machine stitch in the ditches of the blocks, vertically and horizontally; also diagonally across the blocks, accenting the color change within each block. Linda found a gorgeous skein of hand-dyed rayon furry yarn and used it by couching it in a meandering design along the middle of the border. It provided the quilting in the same step and beautifully unified the whole piece.

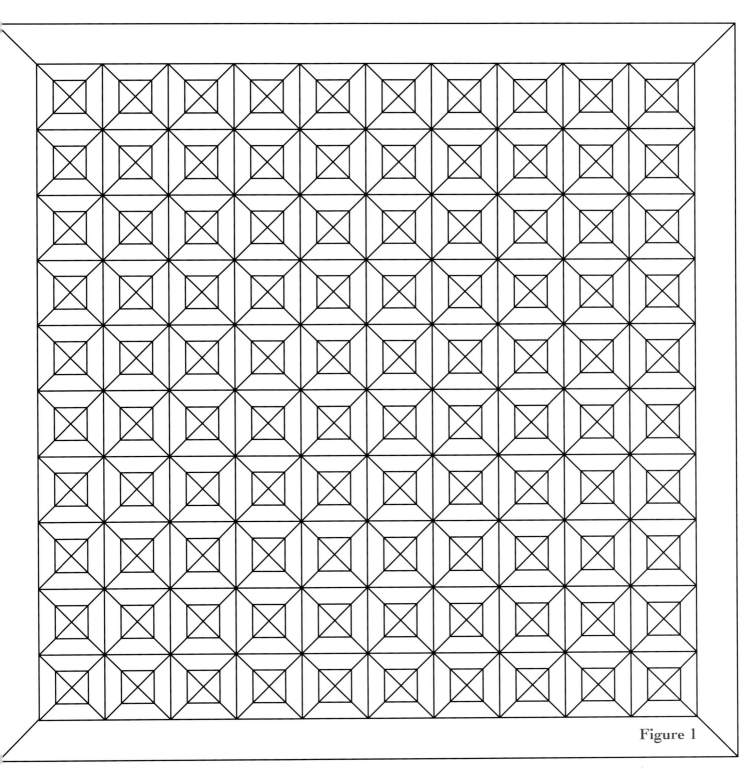

Figure 1

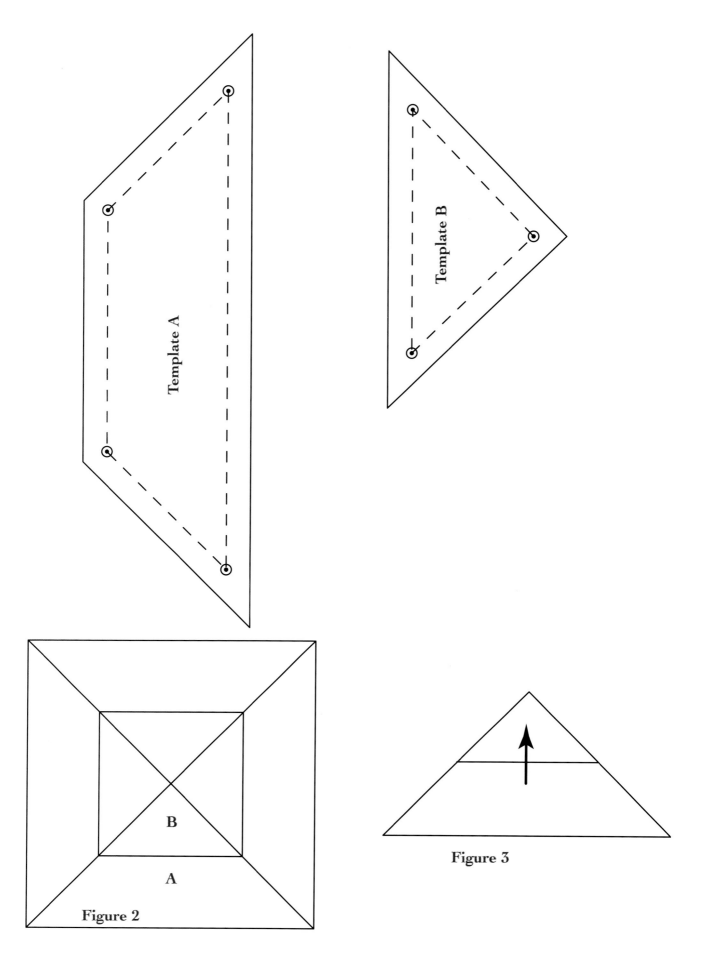

Template A

Template B

Figure 2

A

B

Figure 3

Garden View

(33 1/4" x 46 1/2")
(Advanced)

Joyce Murrin ©2000
Orient, New York

Special fabrics and a few added lines have transformed a simple tulip block into a twenty-first century garden, as viewed through a window. The inspiration for this delightful hanging was *Crossed Tulips*.

Techniques: Machine piecing with hand appliquéd curve; or all pieced by hand or machine. Add seam allowances to all templates. Arrows indicate suggested straight-of-grain placement.

Fabrics: Hand dyed, batik cottons, and commercial "look-a-likes"

Approximate yardage and cutting:
- Twenty-four, 2/3 yard <u>bright</u> green for block corners (Template A)
- Six, 8" x 12" pieces of <u>medium</u> pink, peach, blue, and purple (Template B)
- Twenty-four, 1/3 yard <u>medium</u> olive green for foliage (Template C)
- Six, 5" x 16" pieces of <u>light</u> pink, peach, blue, and purple (Template D)
- Six, 5" x 16" pieces of <u>dark</u> pink, peach, blue, and purple (Template D <u>reversed</u>)
- Twenty-four, 1/3 yard yellow for buds (Template E)
- Six, 1" x 9" <u>bright</u> green (Template F)
- Twenty-four, 1/8 yard slightly darker green (Template G)
- Twenty-four, 1/3 yard sky blue (Template H)
- 1 1/3 yards for sashing and border

Suggestion: To break the "sameness" of the flowers in each block, reverse the light and dark petal positions in several blocks.

Assembly: (Prepare six 12 1/4" blocks)(**Figure 1**)

1. To prepare each tulip unit, stitch together D, B, and D reversed. Press as you go.

2. Join to A and set aside. (Unit 1)

3. Stitch H to E, and add C. Set aside. (Unit 2)

4. Prepare center stem strip by joining G to F and another G. Set aside.

5. On both sides of one G, add a Unit 2 (H, E, and C). Repeat.

6. Piece units to each side of the center stem. The block is complete, except for the corners and tulip section. (Unit 1)

7. Appliqué or piece corner tulip units to block center.

8. Set completed blocks in two vertical rows of three with sashing between blocks. (Finished sashing width is 1 1/8".) Join two rows with one vertical sashing strip.

9. Add 3 1/2" border.

Quilting: Trace the quilting templates onto 1 1/2"-wide masking tape. Position tape, quilt around, and reuse. No marking on the fabric is necessary! See **Figure 2** for placement of motifs. Dotted lines indicate additional quilting tracks.

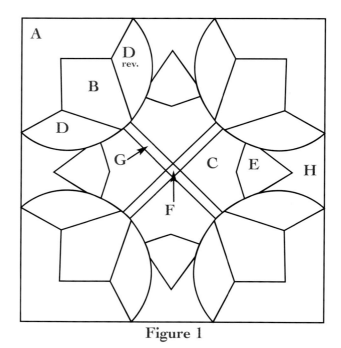

Figure 1

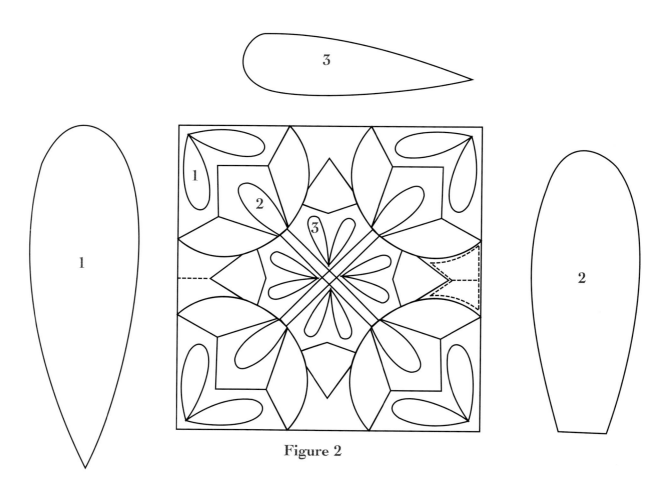

Figure 2

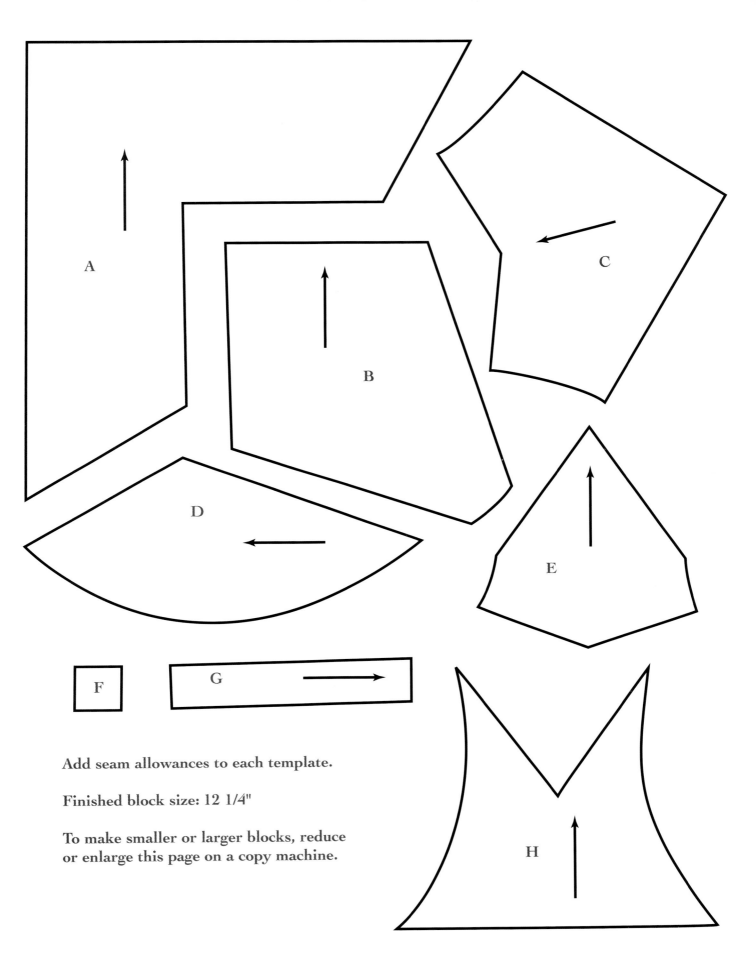

A

B

C

D

E

F

G

H

Add seam allowances to each template.

Finished block size: 12 1/4"

To make smaller or larger blocks, reduce or enlarge this page on a copy machine.

Montanafires.2000

(46.5" x 69")

(Advanced)

Mary Kay Hitchner ©2000
Haverford, Pennsylvania

The horrendous fires of the summer of 2000 inspired this spectacular, quilted wall hanging. The title refers to the Web site that was checked daily to monitor the maker's family property — located much too close to the danger area. The vertical construction was suggested by *Doris Mabel*.

Techniques: Machine piecing; hand appliqué; machine quilting

Fabrics: A variety of hand-painted, marbled, hand-dyed fabrics, Bali prints, and commercial prints (All 100% cotton)

Approximate yardage:
- 1 yard green hand-painted fabric
- 1 yard green/black Bali print for left border
- 1/2 yard (total) of five to six assorted greens
- 1/2 yard "flame-charred" fabric for right border and strips in body of quilt
- 1 yard (total) of fifteen to sixteen assorted "fire" fabrics

- 4 yards fabric for backing, binding, and sleeve

Assembly:

1. Refer to full Gallery photo for suggested fabric placement.

2. Cut fabrics according to personal preference.

3. Audition elements on a design wall.

4. Stitch elements together.

5. Hand appliqué "flame" motifs. See Gallery photo.

Quilting: Machine stitch in the ditches along the vertical strips. Free-motion stitch in larger sections to create the movement of the fire's heat and smoke. Clear monofilament thread was used on the top; lingerie thread was used in the bobbin.

Edge finishing: Apply back-edge binding.

Sarasponda

(66" x 66")
(Advanced)

Judith Thompson ©2000
Wenonah, New Jersey

The happy spinning song *Sarasponda* and the Fossil Fern fabric collection, inspired the contemporary interpretation of the 1860s quilt *Sarah* by Sarah Moore Kinne of Sullivan County, New York. It is a traditional red and green scheme with special emphasis on the chartreuse green.

Techniques: Piecing by hand or machine; appliqué by hand; stem stitch and buttonhole stitch embroidery by hand; hand quilting

Fabric: Fossil Fern Collections by Benartex; fabric by Kona Bay

Approximate yardage:
- 2 1/4 yards chartreuse for background
- 1 1/4 yards peach background

- 1 1/4 yards red for inner border and binding
- Assorted "fat quarters" in green, red, pink, and yellow for appliqué pieces

Assembly: All measurements are finished sizes. Be sure to add seam allowances to appliqué shapes.

1. Cut background pieces for appliqué. See **Figure 1**. Refer to Gallery for full color photo.

a. Center 15" x 15"
b. Center border 6" x 10"
c. Corner triangles 19" x 19" x 27"
d. Outside borders 13" x 40"
e. Corners 13" x 13"

2. Prepare the appliqué pieces, leaves, flowers, and 3/16" bias tubes for stems.

3. Piece four eight-pointed star blocks (8 1/2" x 8 1/2"). (**Figure 2**) Templates include seam allowances.

4. Assemble the center, center border, and star blocks as shown in **Figure 1**.

5. Appliqué the shapes (Flowers A), and embroider the small stems and small flowers on the center panel.

6. Appliqué the shapes (Flowers B) and embroider the flowers to the center border.

7. Stitch the four large triangles to the sides of the inner border.

8. Appliqué the shapes (Flowers C) and embroider them on the corner triangles.

9. Apply 1" inner border.

10. Attach the outside border and corners.

11. Appliqué the shapes (Flowers D) and embroider them on the outside border.

12. Appliqué the shapes (Flowers E) to the corners.

Quilting: Outline all appliqué pieces; fill in the background with a grid, clamshells, or diagonal lines.

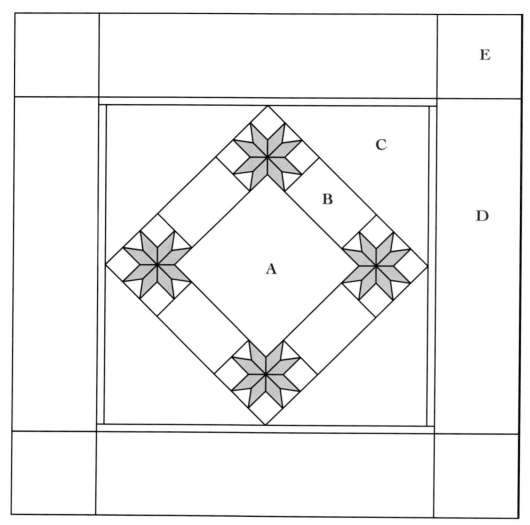

Figure 1

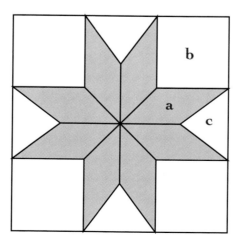

Figure 2

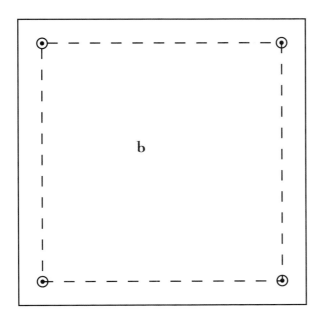

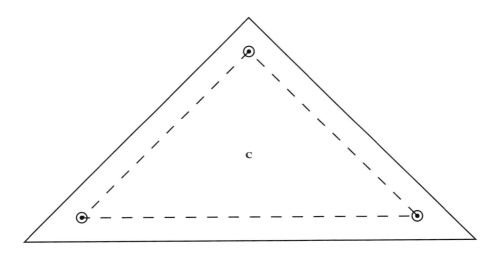

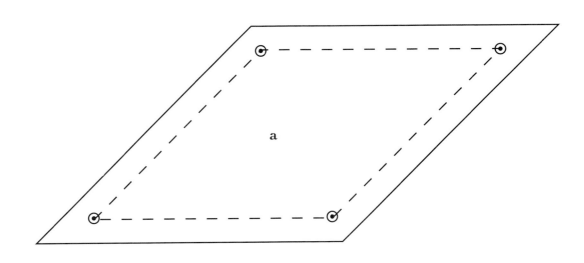

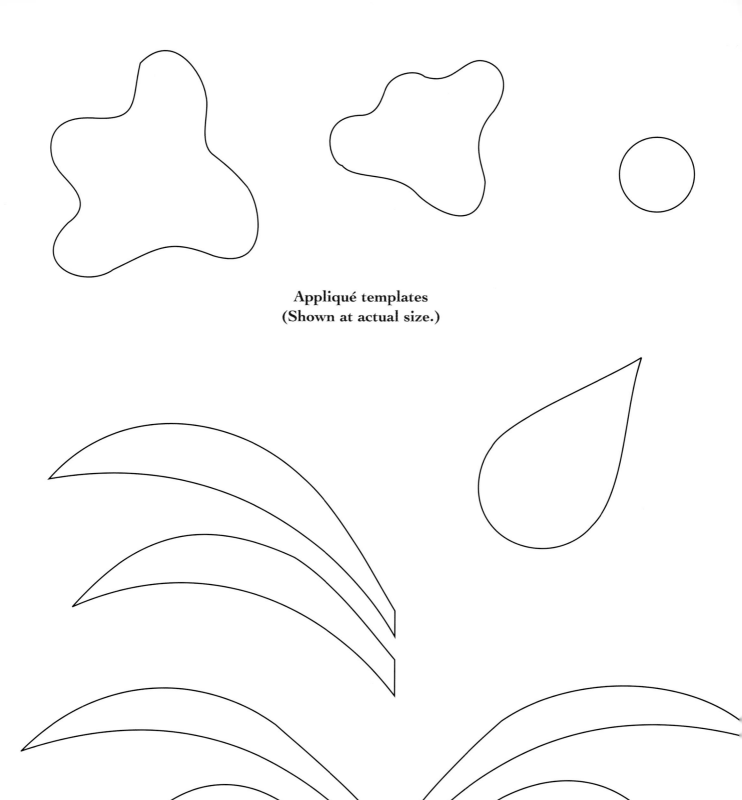

Appliqué templates
(Shown at actual size.)

Center panel A

(Shown at 50% of actual size.)

Inner block B,
6" x 10"

(Shown at 75% of
actual size.)

Corner block C, 19" x 19" x 27"

(Shown at 50% of actual size.)

1/4 of outside border D

(Shown at 50% of actual size.)

1/4 of corner block E, 6 1/2" x 6 1/2"

(Shown at actual size.)

Addendum A: Quiltmakers

Old tops completed by

Jeannette T. Muir (10)
Becky Herdle (2)
Patricia J. Morris
Anita Ringen
Madge Ziegler

New tops made by

Margaret Bowling
Nancy Breland
Linda Hall
Jane Hamilton
Mary Kay Hitchner
Lynn Kough
Carolyn Larason
Merry May
Jeannie Roulet Minchak
Patricia J. Morris
Joyce Murrin
Marion Nicoll
Irene Sherman
Judith Thompson
Madge Ziegler

Addendum B: The names for Jeannette T. Muir's quilts

These quilts are named after Jeannette's relatives and friends.

"Alice Henrietta" Meyer Mason (1924-1996) (friend) Medford, New Jersey

"Doris Mabel" Carpenter Tousley (sister-in-law) Keene, New Hampshire

"Fanny May" Lawson (late 1800s) (great aunt) Burlington, Vermont

"Gwendolyn Julie" Van Lieshout Powell (friend) Merion, Pennsylvania

"Kathlyn Jane" Fender Sullivan (friend) Raleigh, North Carolina

"Lillias" Harris Anderson (friend) Medford, New Jersey

"Lois Margaret" Ravikio McGann (friend) Moorestown, New Jersey

"Lottie" Carrie Arvilla Battles (dec.) ("aunt" friend) Randolph, Vermont

"Maude Isabel" Buss Garrison (friend) Freehold, New Jersey

"Patsy Jean" Pelletier Morris (friend, colleague, co-author) Pitman, New Jersey

American Quilter's Society
P.O. Box 3290
Paducah, KY 42002-3290
E-Mail: info@aqsquilt.com
http://aqsquilt.com
(Certified appraisers, books)

Auntie Em's Attic, Emily Hooper
103 S. Martin
Osage City, KS 66523
(785) 528-4771
(Antique quilts and tops)

Clotilde, Inc.
B 3000
Louisiana, MO 63353-3000
(800) 772-2891 (Credit card orders)
(800) 863-3191 (Fax orders)
(800) 545-4002 (Customer service)
http://www.clotilde.com

Connecting Threads
P.O. Box 8940
Vancouver, WA 98668-8940
(800) 574-6454 (Credit card orders, customer
    service)
(360) 260-8877 (Fax orders)
E-mail: customerservice@connectingthreads.com
http://connectingthreads.com

Crazy Ladies and Friends
1606 Santa Monica Blvd.
Santa Monica, CA 90404
(1" brass pins and other mail order)

Diane Reese
4 Powhatan Rd.
Pepperell, MA 01463
(Antique quilts and tops)

Fairfield Processing Corporation
P.O. Box 1157
Danbury, CT 06810
http://www.fairfieldprocessing.com
(Batting)

Julia Bright Antiques
1349 West Wood St.
Decatur, IL 62522
(Antique quilts and tops)

Keepsake Quilting
Rt. 25B, P.O. Box 1618
Centre Harbor, NH 03226-1618
(800) 525-8086
(603) 253-8346 (Fax orders)
E-mail: keepsake@worldpath.net
http://www.keepsakequilting.com
(Mail order)

Merikay Waldvogel
1501 Whittower Rd.
Knoxville, TN 37919
(Author, curator, lecturer)

Moto Photo and Portrait Studio
Paul and Connie Ferrigno, owners
Kings Highway and Lenola Road
Maple Shade, NJ 08052
(856) 235-6684

Mountain Mist Quilt Center
The Stearns Technical Textiles Co.
100 Williams St.
Cincinnati, OH 45215-4683
(800) 345-7150
(513) 948-5281 (Fax orders)
E-mail: mountain.mist@stearnstextiles.com
http://www.stearnstextiles.com/mountainmist
(Batting and patterns)

Nancy's Notions
P.O. Box 683
333 Biechl Ave.
Beaver Dam, WI 53916-0683
(800) 245-5116 (Customer service)
(800) 833-0690 (Credit card orders)
(800) 255-8119 (Fax orders)
E-mail: news@nancysnotions.com
http://www.nancysnotions.com

Quilts and Other Comforts
B 2500
Louisiana, MO 63353-7500
(800) 881-6624 (Credit card orders)
(800) 418-3326 (Customer service)
(888) 886-7196 (Fax orders)
E-mail: qoc.address@starkbros.com
http://www.quiltsonline.com

The Stencil Company
28 Castlewood Dr.
Cheektowaga, NY 14227
(716) 656-9430 (Customer service)
(716) 668-2488 (Fax orders)
E-mail: info@quiltingstencils.com
http://quiltingstencils.com
(Quilting stencils)

Treadleart
25834 Narbonne Ave.
Lomita, CA 90717
(310) 534-5122
E-mail: treadleart@treadleart.com
http://treadleart.com

Vintage Textiles and Tools
P.O. Box 265
Merion, PA 19066
(Antique tools, tops, quilts, and other collectibles)

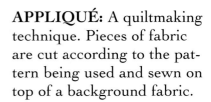

ADVANCED: Projects that require a degree of technical skill beyond the basic. Not for novice quiltmakers.

ALTERNATING BLOCKS: Set option. Solid, print, or pieced blocks used to separate other patterned blocks.

APPLIQUÉ: A quiltmaking technique. Pieces of fabric are cut according to the pattern being used and sewn on top of a background fabric.

APPRAISAL: Valuation of a quilt, top, or blocks by a knowledgeable individual. Can be done for insurance, resale, donation, or general information purposes.

AUDITION: Placing the quilt units on a design wall to determine visual impact. The units can be moved around until, upon a critical viewing, the best possible layout is achieved.

BACKGROUND: Fabric on which appliqué pieces are stitched.

BACKING: Bottom layer of a quilt (lining). It may be solid, pieced, or in any other way patterned. Fiber content should be consistent with that of the top.

BASIC: Fundamental techniques of quiltmaking are employed—the least difficult of the projects.

BASTING: That which holds the three layers of the quilt sandwich together on a temporary basis while the quilting is being done. Basting can be done with thread stitching or safety pins.

BATIK: An Indonesian style fabric created by coating with wax parts not to be dyed.

BATTING: The soft inner layer (filler) of the quilt. Depending on the item being prepared, and personal preference, the quiltmaker may choose cotton, polyester blend, or wool batt. Thin cotton batting was most commonly used in old quilts.

BIAS: The diagonal grain of the fabric compared to the straight and cross grain.

BINDING: One method, and perhaps the most common, of finishing the edges of a quilt. The binding can be bias grain, cross grain, or straight of the grain. Double-fold binding is generally preferred.

BLANKET STITCH: Embroidery stitch that can be used both for securing appliqué pieces on a background and for decorative purposes. May be an open or closed stitch.

BLENDS: Those fabrics that are a combination of natural (cotton) and man-made fibers. Sometimes fabric made entirely of man-made fibers is

called a blend, as is the combination of two or more natural fibers.

BLOCK: A single design unit, usually a square, repeated to make up the quilt top.

BORDER: Outermost element(s) of the constructed quilt top—exclusive of the binding. Generally it is thought of as a frame for the piece.

CLEAN FINISH: Squaring up the sides and corners, and cutting off the debris.

COMFORTER: Thick textile sandwich, usually tied, not quilted. May be pieced or plain.

COMPATIBLE (color and fiber content): Elements that coexist and work together to provide harmony to the piece.

CONTEMPORARY: All items that are from one specific period—be that period current or ancient.

CONTINUOUS-LINE QUILTING TRACKS: Unbroken lines stitched with minimal starts and stops. Ideally these lines begin and end at the edge of the project.

COPYRIGHT: The exclusive legal right to reproduce, publish, and sell works—be they in written or fiber form.

COTTON: Fabric of good-quality, medium-weight, natural fiber preferred for quiltmaking. Should not be too loosely or tightly woven, too heavy or thin, or slippery.

COW MAGNETS: Strong, high-density magnets used to retrieve dropped needles or pins.

CUTTER: An old quilt top which, instead of being restored, is cut up to make vests, bears, or other boutique items. The authors deplore this practice.

DESIGN WALL: Ample vertical surface on which quilt design elements can be attached for previewing/auditioning purposes.

DITCH: Area in a pieced quilt that runs directly along a seam line on the side away from which the seam allowances have been pressed. Also, the area in an appliqué quilt that is immediately outside of an appliqué unit.

DOCUMENTATION: Furnishing, or authenticating, a quilt with the use of documents. Can be through historical documents or objective facts.

EDGE FINISHING: Method used to complete the outside edges of the textile sandwich.

EMBELLISHMENTS: Ornaments, found items, etc., applied to the quilt to enhance and complement the design.

EMBROIDERY: Process of forming decorative designs with hand or machine needlework. May also be used for construction purposes.

ENGLISH PIECING: A quiltmaking technique. It involves basting fabric onto paper templates then holding the basted units together and whip stitching them to each other. After sewing is completed, the paper templates are removed.

FEEDSACKS: Cotton fabric, coarsely woven, either patterned or plain, used to store grain, feed, or household staples.

FOUNDATION: Base fabric used for stabilization when employing certain quiltmaking techniques. When the project is completed, foundation is totally covered or removed.

FREE-MOTION QUILTING: A process of machine quilting done with the feed dogs dropped.

FREEZER PAPER: Used to facilitate both piecing and appliqué techniques.

FUSSY CUT: Requires the use of a template to cut exactly the same motif for repetitive use.

GRAIN: Refers to the threads of the fabric. Straight grain is

parallel to the selvage and has the least amount of give. Cross grain is perpendicular to the selvage and has a small amount of give. True bias is at a 45-degree angle to the selvage and has the most give.

HAND CREAM: Lotion used to protect and improve the skin while working with fabric, threads, and paper. Should be quickly and thoroughly absorbed, thus Udder Cream is recommended.

HAND-DYES: Specially dyed (or over-dyed) fabric.

HEIRLOOM: An item of value, intrinsically or sentimentally, that is passed down from generation to generation.

INNOVATIVE: That which is done in a new or different manner. Refers to both aesthetic and technical phases of quiltmaking.

INTERMEDIATE: Skills that are beyond the basic, but are not quite up to those required for advanced projects.

MASTER TEMPLATE: Pattern that is reproduced a number of times for the project.

MEDALLION: Set option. Central portion of a quilt surrounded by multiple blocks and/or borders.

MOTIF: Repeated design element. Can also refer to the design appearing and repeating in the fabric being used.

MUSEUM-QUALITY: A work that is worthy of museum display because of its use of good fabrics, fine points of construction, overall good manipulation of color and value, and excellent state of preservation.

MUSLIN: Medium-weight cotton fabric. Can be unbleached (the most common), bleached or dyed.

NON-PHOSPHATE DETERGENT: Neutral, synthetic detergent that rinses away freely.

ON POINT: Set option. Refers to the orientation of the blocks. Straight of grain runs vertically from point to opposite point.

PAPER FOUNDATION PIECING: A quiltmaking technique. A pattern is reproduced on paper—one for each block or unit needed. The fabrics are then stitched to each other and through the lines on the pattern. After all sewing is completed, the paper pattern is removed.

PATCHWORK: A quiltmaking technique. Can apply to appliqué, but more commonly refers to pieced work.

PICKER: An item (quilt, top, or blocks) purchased with the intention of completely disassembling it in order to remake the piece or to use it in other renovation projects.

PIECING: A quiltmaking technique. The sewing of one piece of fabric to another to create a large piece of constructed fabric.

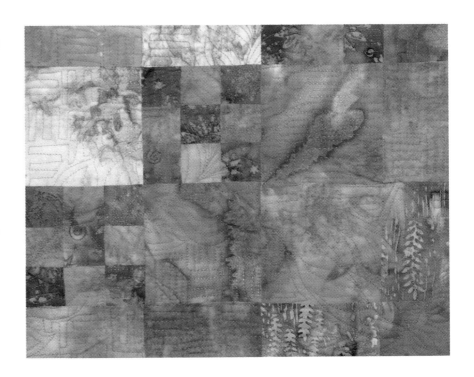

PIN-UP WALL: Same as design wall.

PLACEMENT SKETCH: Drawing of the quilt top's planned layout.

POST: Areas (usually square) that fall at the intersections of the sashing.

PRAIRIE POINTS: Decorative edging for a quilt using inserted folded triangles. Also occasionally used on the interior of the top for decorative purposes.

PRECISION PIECING: Accurate method of construction. Templates are used, and stitching is done on the marked lines.

PROVENANCE: Covers the origin and source of an item as well as the "road" it has traveled before reaching your hands. This can include dates, names of people, and names of places.

PUBLIC DOMAIN: Refers to items where property rights are not protected by copyright and whose use is free to everyone.

QUICK PIECING: Cutting is done in layers—usually with a rotary cutter—without a template, and material is then chain pieced.

QUILT: The most commonly used definition is "textile sandwich," a term coined by Patsy and Myron Orlofsky.

QUILTING: A quiltmaking technique. The execution of small, even-running stitches that hold together the three layers of the quilt and provide an additional design element to the work.

RECONSTRUCTION: The remaking of an item to get rid of as many of its flaws and problems as possible.

RENOVATION: Generally speaking, the restoration of the good shape the item formerly had.

REPAIR: All things that are done to a damaged quilt, top, or block to fix the item and make it possible to complete and use it.

REPRODUCTION: An item that is made to be as close as possible to the piece you are copying.

ROTARY CUTTER: A sharp tool used to cut fabric.

REPRODUCTION FABRICS (REPRO FABRICS): Fabrics being produced today that replicate fabrics from other time periods.

SAMPLER: A quilt or wall hanging consisting of a variety of quilt blocks—each one different—set together in one top. Students frequently make samplers in basic courses. Many teachers find samplers valuable as teaching and learning tools.

SANDWICH: Refers to the quilt and its three layers: The top, batting, and backing. The quilt sandwich is held together by quilting, or, in some cases, tying.

SASHING: Set option. Strips of fabric sewn between and separating blocks in a quilt top. Strips may be solid or pieced. Also called lattice or stripping.

SAWTOOTH: Pieced half-triangles that form a decorative element and are often used just inside a plain, outer border.

SEAM ALLOWANCE: That 1/4" of fabric that lies outside the sewing line in piecing. It is not stitched down during the precision piecing technique. In appliqué, the seam allowance is turned under the pieces being applied either before beginning the appliqué work or during the process.

SELVAGE or SELVEDGE: Lengthwise, woven edge of the fabric. Should be removed before the fabric is used.

SET: Layout of the quilt top design elements. There are many possible varieties and combinations of sets such as Sashed, On Point, and Block to Block.

SLEEVE: A tube of fabric that is sewn to the top of the quilt back, and—with a dowel, rod, or lath inserted—enables the quilt to be hung for display.

STIPPLE: The design of the quilting stitch.

STRIPPIE: Set option. Vertical bands of piecing or appliqué alternating with long sashing strips.

TEMPLATE: A firm pattern that is placed on the fabric and around which the cutting/sewing lines are marked and stitched. Generally, lightweight plastic is the most satisfactory material, although cardboard (not corrugated) or other material can be used.

TESSELLATION: Mosaic-like design using shapes that fit together without leaving a space or overlapping.

TIED QUILTS: Quilts/comforters of three layers that are held together with square knots or bows instead of, or in addition to, quilting stitches.

TOP: Upper layer of the quilt, containing the design elements.

TRADITIONAL: Quilts made using designs that are in the public domain and

passed down from generation to generation.

UNIT: Repeated portion of a block. Can also refer to the entire block.

VINTAGE: Those items that are from the same time period.

ZIGZAG: Set option. Uses large setting triangles to separate the pattern blocks.

Beyer, Jinny. *Patchwork Patterns*. McLean, Va.: EPM Publications, Inc, 1979.

———. *The Quilter's Album of Blocks and Borders*. McLean, Va.: EPM Publications, Inc., 1980.

Brackman, Barbara. *Clues in the Calico: A Guide to Identifying and Dating Old Quilts*. McLean, Va.: EPM Publications, Inc., 1989.

———. *Encyclopedia of Appliqué: An Illustrated, Numerical Index to Traditional and Modern Patterns*. McLean, Va.: EPM Publications, Inc., 1993.

———. *Encyclopedia of Pieced Quilt Patterns*. Paducah, Ky.: American Quilter's Society, 1993.

Chandler, Elizabeth and Joanne Donahue. *Quilting Designs from Grandma's Attic*. Evansville, Ind.: Lizanne Publishing Company, 1994.

Cochran, Rachel, Rita Erickson, Natalie Hart, and Barbara Schaffer. *New Jersey Quilts 1777-1950: Contributions to an American Tradition*. Paducah, Ky.: American Quilter's Society, 1992.

Dietrich, Mimi. *Quilts from The Smithsonian: 12 Designs Inspired by the Textile Collection of The National Museum of American History*. Bothwell, Wash.: That Patchwork Place, 1995.

Hargrave, Harriet. *Heirloom Machine Quilting*. Westminster, Calif.: Burdett Publications, 1987.

Haywood, Dixie. "Picking, Ripping, and other Reverse Sewing." *Quilter's Newsletter Magazine*. Issue 312 (May 1999): 32-33.

Herdle, Becky. *Time-Span Quilts: New Quilts from Old Tops*. Paducah, Ky.: American Quilter's Society, 1994.

Kough, Lynn G. *Quiltmaking for Beginners: A Stitch by Stitch Guide*. San Francisco: Quilt Digest Press, 2000.

McElroy, Roxanne. *That Perfect Stitch: The Secrets of Fine Hand Quilting*. Chicago: The Quilt Digest Press, 1998.

Morris, Patricia J. *The Ins and Outs: Perfecting the Quilting Stitch*. Paducah, Ky.: American Quilter's Society, 1990.

———. *The Judge's Task: How Award Winning Quilts are Selected*. Paducah, Ky.: American Quilter's Society, 1993.

——— and Jeannette T. Muir. *Worth Doing Twice: Creating Quilts from Old Tops*. Iola, Wis.: Krause Publications, 1999.

Muir, Jeannette Tousley. *Precision Patchwork for Scrap Quilts: Anytime, Anywhere...* Paducah Ky.: American Quilter's Society, 1995.

Nephew, Sara. *My Mother's Quilts: Designs from the Thirties.* Bothell, Wash.: That Patchwork Place, Inc., 1988.

Newman, Sharon. *Making Quilts from Vintage Blocks,* bk. 1 of *Treasures from Yesteryear.* Bothell, Wash.: That Patchwork Place, Inc., 1995.

———. *Replicating Antique Quilts,* bk. 2 of *Treasures from Yesteryear.* Bothell, Wash.: That Patchwork Place, Inc., 1995.

Orlofsky, Patsy and Myron Orlofsky. *Quilts in America.* New York: McGraw-Hill Book Co., 1974.

Pahl, Ellen, ed. *The Quiltmaker's Ultimate Visual Guide.* Emmaus, Pa.: Rodale Press, Inc., 1997. (Jeannette T. Muir, contributor.)

Roy, Gerald E. *Quilts by Paul D. Pilgrim: Blending the Old & the New.* Paducah, Ky.: American Quilter's Society, 1997.

Soltys, Karen Costello, ed. *Fast and Fun Machine Quilting.* Emmaus, Pa.: Rodale Press, Inc., 1997. (Jeannette T. Muir, contributor.)

Stearns & Foster Catalogue of Quilt Pattern Designs and Needle Craft Supplies. Cincinnati, Ohio: Stearns and Foster, n.d.

Townswick, Jane. *Easy Machine Quilting.* Emmaus, Pa.: Rodale Press, Inc., 1996. (Jeannette T. Muir, contributor.)

Trestain, Eileen Jahnke. *Dating Fabrics: A Color Guide 1880-1960.* Paducah, Ky.: American Quilter's Society, 1998.

Wagner, Debra. *Teach Yourself Machine Piecing and Quilting.* Radnor, Pa.: Chilton Book Co., 1992.

———. *Traditional Quilts, Today's Techniques.* Iola, Wis.: Krause Publications, 1997.

Waldvogel, Merikay. *Soft Covers for Hard Times: Quiltmaking & the Great Depression.* Nashville, Tenn.: Rutledge Hill Press, 1990.

——— and Barbara Brackman. *Patchwork Souvenirs of the 1933 World's Fair.* Nashville, Tenn.: Rutledge Hill Press, 1993.

Woodard, Thos. K. and Blanche Greenstein. *Twentieth Century Quilts: 1900-1950.* New York: E.P. Dutton, 1988.

Index

Learn from the Experts

Kaye Wood's Strip-Cut Quilts
by Kaye Wood
Learn timesaving techniques for accurate cutting and quilting with renowned quilter Kaye Wood. Explore the many triangle shapes that can be cut with the Starmaker® 8 Master Template including horizontal and vertical cuts, fussy cuts, flying geese, trees and many more. Use these shapes to create 25 beautiful projects including quilts, wall hangings, and table runners.

Softcover • 8-1/4 x 10-7/8
96 pages
200 illustrations • 30 color photos
Item# KWNSQ • $19.95

Snippet Sensations
by Cindy Walter
Using fusible fabric, Cindy Walter walks you through this easy, fun, no-sew technique, allowing you to "paint" with fabric. Now beautiful works of art can be created with fabric scraps! Included are more than 50 color Snippet photographs and three step-by-step projects to introduce you to the wonderful world of Snippets.

Softcover • 8-1/4 x 10-7/8
96 pages
90 color photos
Item# SNIP • $19.95

Worth Doing Twice
Creating Quilts from Old Tops
by Patricia J. Morris and Jeannette T. Muir
Details the renovation and reconstruction of old quilt tops, dating from the 1870s to the 1940s, providing you with valuable information on where to find old quilt tops and how to repair, stitch, and finish them. Before and after photos, as well as step-by-step instructions for 20 designs, guide you through the process of finishing a quilt from the days of old or mending a quilt in need of repairs.

Softcover • 8-1/4 x 10-7/8
128 pages
117 illustrations and 59 color photos
Item# WDT • $19.95

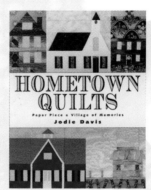

Hometown Quilts
Paper Piece a Village of Memories
by Jodie Davis
Create your own hometown quilt using paper piecing and any combination of the 27 block patterns included in this easy-to-follow book. Complete step-by-step illustrated instructions and full-size patterns are used to teach paper piece quilting. Clear layout diagrams and beautiful color photographs will inspire you to create a quilt from the book, or come up with your own village of memories.

Softcover • 8-1/4 x 10-7/8
128 pages
50 color photos
Item# MEMQU • $21.95

Attic Windows
Quilts With a View, 2nd Edition
by Diana Leone & Cindy Walter
Attic Windows is a timeless technique for quilters of all ages and skill levels to use their imagination, creativity, and favorite motif fabrics. Now in full color, this comprehensive volume contains a gallery of more than 50 inspiring Attic Window quilts, information on selecting fabrics, tips on how to use colors effectively, and numerous exercises to help you plan a one-of-a-kind quilt.

Softcover • 8-1/4 x 10-7/8
96 pages
20 illustrations • 100 color photos
Item# ATWI • $19.95

Fine Hand Quilting
2nd Edition
by Diana Leone & Cindy Walter
The art of hand quilting is given the royal treatment in this completely revised second edition of the most respected book on the topic. World-renown authors and teachers Diana Leone and Cindy Walter have tested all of the latest tools and materials on the market, provided tried-and-true techniques so you can create even stitches, and included three projects to get you started right away! This full-color update also has tips from quilting pros, a special section on "How to Quilt This Quilt," and a gallery of gorgeous, inspirational quilts.

Softcover • 8-1/4 x 10-7/8
112 pages
150 color photos
Item# FHQU • $19.95